Series/Number 07-161

DIFFERENTIAL ITEM FUNCTIONING, SECOND EDITION

Steven J. Osterlind

University of Missouri–Columbia

Howard T. Everson

Center for Advanced Study in Education, City University of New York

Los Angeles | London | New Delhi
Singapore | Washington DC

For information:

SAGE Publications, Inc.
2455 Teller Road
Thousand Oaks,
 California 91320
E-mail: order@sagepub.com

SAGE Publications Ltd.
1 Oliver's Yard
55 City Road
London EC1Y 1SP
United Kingdom

SAGE Publications India Pvt. Ltd.
B 1/I 1 Mohan Cooperative
 Industrial Area
Mathura Road, New Delhi 110 044
India

SAGE Publications Asia-Pacific
 Pte. Ltd.
33 Pekin Street #02-01
Far East Square
Singapore 048763

Printed in the United States of America

Library of Congress Cataloging-in-Publication Data

Osterlind, Steven J.
Differential item functioning/Steven J. Osterlind, Howard T. Everson.—2nd ed.
 p. cm.—(Quantitative applications in the social sciences; 161)
Revised ed. of: Test item bias.
Includes bibliographical references and index.
ISBN 978-1-4129-5494-5 (pbk.: acid-free paper)
 1. Social sciences—Statistical methods. 2. Social sciences—Methodology.
I. Everson, Howard T. II. Osterlind, Steven J. Test item bias. III. Title.

HA29.O79 2009
519.5'2—dc22   2008049934

This book is printed on acid-free paper.

09   10   11   12   13   10   9   8   7   6   5   4   3   2   1

Acquisitions Editor:	Vicki Knight
Associate Editor:	Lauren Habib
Editorial Assistant:	Ashley Dodd
Production Editor:	Brittany Bauhaus
Copy Editor:	QuADS PrePress (P) Ltd.
Typesetter:	C&M Digitals (P) Ltd.
Proofreader:	Sally Jaskold
Indexer:	Diggs Publication Services, Inc.
Cover Designer:	Candice Harman
Marketing Manager:	Karen Ehrmann

CONTENTS

ABOUT THE AUTHORS

Steven J. Osterlind, PhD, is Professor of Measurement and Statistics and Director of Educational Psychology program, University of Missouri–Columbia. His expertise is in psychological assessment, including tests and measurement, statistics, psychometric methods, and test development. At the University of Missouri, he teaches graduate-level courses in multivariate statistics, analysis of variance, regression, general linear modeling, and psychometric methods. Additionally, he teaches seminar courses on specialized topics, including item response theory and computer applications of testing. He has worked on numerous national testing programs, including serving as statistician for NAEP (National Assessment of Educational Progress). In licensing and certification, he has worked with dozens of professional associations and organizations on their assessment programs. He has authored five books, the most recent of which is a major textbook titled *Modern Measurement: Theory, Principles, and Application of Mental Appraisal,* and he has written more than 60 articles, book chapters, and other research reports in assessment. Additionally, he has authored more than 20 tests. He is principal author of *College Basic Academic Subjects Examination* (C-BASE), a test of collegiate achievement currently adopted by more than 100 universities across the nation. He received his doctoral degree in 1976 in educational psychology (measurement and statistics) from the University of Southern California. In 1979, he was an American Scholar's Fellow at Yale University.

Howard T. Everson, PhD, is currently Senior Research Fellow at the Center for Advanced Study in Education, at the Graduate Center, City University of New York. In addition, he serves as a consulting research scientist to the American Institutes for Research and the American Councils for International Education. His research and scholarly interests focus on the intersection of cognition, instruction, and assessment. He has contributed to developments in educational psychology, psychometrics, and quantitative methods. Before joining the faculty at the City University of New York, he was a professor of Psychology and Psychometrics at Fordham University. In addition, Dr. Everson was the executive director of the NAEP Education

Statistics Services Institute at the American Institutes for Research and is a former vice president for Research at the College Board. He is a fellow of both the American Educational Research Association and the American Psychological Association.

SERIES EDITOR'S INTRODUCTION

Broadly speaking, there are two tasks for quantitative research in the social sciences. First and foremost, the social scientist wants to capture a particular social phenomenon with a measurement that corresponds to a conceptualization of the phenomenon. Furthermore, the researcher often aims to understand this social phenomenon with some kind of explanatory statistical model so that a deeper knowledge is gained from the model as to what may have led to the occurrence of the observed phenomenon.

The overwhelming majority of the volumes in our series fall in the two categories of measurement and modeling (perhaps, with more belonging to the second than to the first group), other than the few numbers on mathematical and statistical basics or on a different mode of inquiry, say the volume on agent-based modeling (even there, a thorough understanding of measurement *and* modeling is still essential for constructing valid agent-based models).

The history of measurement goes back a long way to prehistorical times when humans needed to measure for living—such as constructing dwellings, making clothes, and bartering and trading food and goods for subsistence. Sometimes, measurement was involved for purposes beyond basic survival: No doubt, Stonehenge could not have been built without some good enough measurement. Measurement efforts akin to what we do in the social sciences today were much more recent: John Graunt's publication of *Natural and Political Observations Made Upon the Bills of Mortality* (1662) can be said to be the first serious effort to measure patterns of human survival; a good understanding of what it takes to construct useful measures in education and psychology was even more recent. It was not until 1904 that Edward Thorndike saw the unavoidable ambiguity in counting correctly spelled words in measuring spelling ability, however indicative such a frequency might be.

It goes without saying that measurement (or testing in education and educational psychology) is extremely central in social scientific inquiry. It should also be clear why measurement is so important to our series. Since Osterlind's earlier book in the series published in 1983, *Test Item Bias*, a lot of developments have occurred. Even the term *test bias* may not be very adequate anymore for describing the field today. That is why Osterlind and Everson have written the current book, *Differential Item Functioning*, which is much more than a simple update of the 1983 book. Even the term *differential item functioning* takes on a broader connotation than the old term *test item bias*. Simply put, differential item functioning refers to the situation where differences exist in the way a test item functions across certain *social* groups (such as race, gender, and class) matched on the attribute measured by the test item. It is thus evident that the method, albeit centrally located in education and psychology, has a broad social science appeal as well.

This book is a timely update to the old topic as well as a new addition about what has evolved and developed to the series. Osterlind and Everson review in this book a range of differential item functioning statistics—from a form of the Mantel-Haenszel test, to a likelihood ratio test, to an application of the logistic regression, which is introduced in many of the volumes in the series as a means for explanatory modeling instead of a method for assessing measurement as in the current case. While the book is mainly targeted to education and psychology, from a measurement point of view, readers in the broader social sciences may, too, find it of interest.

—*Tim F. Liao*
Series Editor

CHAPTER 1. INTRODUCTION

This monograph replaces *Test Item Bias* (Osterlind, 1983), which appeared in 1983 as #30 in this series (i.e., *Quantitative Applications in the Social Sciences* [QASS]). Psychometric investigation of performance on test items by different, identifiable groups of a population has undergone such dramatic and important change in the past 25 years that merely updating the earlier publication would be inadequate. Not only have the techniques of item inquiry changed (with some former ones now discarded and new processes invented), but more important, the very notion of "item bias" has been completely reevaluated. Today, the relevant studies are generally conducted from a much broader perspective than were those based on the earlier, single term. Now we attend to notions of test fairness and of group invariance in construct representation, as well as to differential item functioning (DIF). Furthermore, some researchers are even formulating strategies to allow for empirically identifying the *causes* of differential performance between groups (see Allalouf, Hambleton, & Sireci, 1999; Roussos & Stout, 1996). With this in mind, we see that DIF is not just a relabeling of "test item bias" in more sensitive language. It is a broad-based phenomenon in assessment, covering diverse aspects of mental appraisal, and it carries with it numerous, consequential implications for both test development and test use. It is part of an open investigation into test and item functioning.

Working from this broader point of view of DIF, our primary goal in this monograph is to present to interested readers current thinking and research about DIF and related concepts, specifically identifying what DIF is, addressing a host of concomitant issues, and then offering an introduction to a variety of statistical procedures useful for researching the DIF phenomenon. Our intention is to assist in learning extensively about DIF techniques, although, of course, the topic is much too large to suggest that this single monograph is comprehensive. No single publication could accomplish that; and accordingly, throughout this work, we reference other sources useful for learning even more about measurement bias, item bias, and DIF detection. This is indeed a large and fertile field, and the related literature is voluminous and continues to grow.

Audience and Requisite Background

The audience for this monograph comprises scholars, test developers, students, and others who may be interested in learning about this particular

1

aspect of test and item performance. Since most strategies useful for researching DIF are statistically based, understanding them requires a solid grounding in both descriptive and inferential statistics. And readers should come to this table with a grasp of variance procedures, such as ANOVA (analysis of variance), ANCOVA (analysis of covariance), and their multivariate analogs (i.e., MANOVA, MANCOVA). Familiarity with correlations and associated procedures is clearly necessary. A working familiarity with the family of regression procedures is requisite to DIF research, particularly with regard to procedures of logistic regression. Furthermore, since much information is expressed most accurately by a formula, readers should be comfortable with deciphering them. When necessary, we explain the terms of a given formula, although we employ common notation throughout. Then, too, readers should know the elements of probability theory and its expression in likelihood functions, as these figure prominently in several DIF detection procedures, such as those based on item response theory as well as on logistic regression. Finally, and importantly, we presume that readers have a strong background in both classical test theory (i.e., true score theory; CTT) and item response theory (IRT), including not only the techniques but also the attendant assumptions. While this requisite background may sound formidable, we realize that there is a large readership who already possess such knowledge, skills, and abilities; and the number of such persons is ever growing.

DIF Remedies in Context

Later on, we do discuss some remedies when DIF is detected; however, from the outset, we caution that the phenomenon is a complex one and to one degree or another may exist in many educational and psychological measures, even when they are carefully and knowledgeably prepared. Because DIF is a common phenomenon, one should not be drawn to the conclusion that if there is DIF, then a test—or tests in general—is unfair or biased. The phenomenon is too complex and ubiquitous in mental measurement for such a simple statement. Nor should its results be summarily discarded.

Furthermore, to suggest that any item exhibiting DIF by some detection strategy should be immediately swept off the test and thereby believe that the test is now made better is simply and plainly incorrect. Such a view would be beyond naïve—closer to ignorant. Sometimes test items exhibiting DIF should be discarded, but just as often, they may be revised or even left alone. We emphasize that the DIF phenomenon is complex, and one should have a sophisticated—even wise—understanding before one approaches questions of how to address it in a given testing situation.

Role of DIF Investigation

The primary purpose for using DIF methods in broad investigations of test items and how they function is quite specific: DIF centers on identifying whether examinee responses to particular test items or sets of test items are linked systematically to the personal characteristics (such as gender or ethnicity) of the examinees and are otherwise unrelated to the test's central construct. Investigating DIF, we argue, allows for a thorough evaluation of a test item with an expectation that the measure may be improved or that a test's score(s) may be interpreted more precisely. Realize, however, that DIF is not designed to reveal true group differences in the appraised or measured construct. After all, estimating true differences is the purpose for an appraisal in the first place.

Primarily, DIF investigations inform test validity. DIF studies, as we said earlier, aid in validating the proposed interpretations of the test scores and thereby permit an evaluation of the claims made on the basis of those scores (Kane, 2006). Indeed, the *Standards for Educational and Psychological Testing* (American Educational Research Association, American Psychological Association, & National Council on Measurement in Education, 1999) usefully and forcefully instruct us that validity is the foremost concern of test development and use and that evidence from many sources—including, obviously, DIF analyses—is required for meaningful, appropriate, and useful interpretation of a test's scores. Thus, DIF evidence contributes to validity in a number of ways, such as when one is developing and evaluating a test or using the test's scores in a decision-making framework—for example, for selection into an educational program or for employment, or to certify a candidate for licensure.

Fairness and DIF

In contemporary conceptions of DIF, issues of *fairness* are prominent. We mention the essence of fairness and DIF here only briefly and discuss it fully later on. It is easiest to grasp the notion of test fairness when contemplating how a test's scores are used in making a particular decision. Of course, using test scores for decision making is the raison d'être for cognitive appraisals, and a thorough appreciation of fairness is precursory to understanding DIF in mental measurement. Applying a test-based decision fairly, however, is likely a principal reason. A decision made with knowledge of the context and probable consequences is usually wise, too. Hence, fairness is not simply sensitivity to affected persons but is also tied to the human attribute of wisdom.

There is a legal context for fairness, too. Its genesis in the United States is the Fourteenth Amendment to our Constitution. Ratified in 1868, it provides that "no state shall . . . deny to any person within its jurisdiction the equal protection of the laws." This amendment ratifies a commitment to the proposition that "all men are created equal," an intention with direct and obvious implication for DIF. More recently, issues of fairness were emphasized by the Civil Rights Act of 1964 and regularly reauthorized. Legal scholars have found wide application of civil rights laws to test fairness. Camilli (2006) chronicles the history of fairness legislation as it pertains to tests.

Bias and DIF

Test bias occurs when a decision, grounded to some degree by the scores yielded from a test, is unfair or has a perceived disparate impact on one group or another. Critics of standardized testing, for example, often point to score differences on mathematics tests for boys and girls as a sign of test bias. *Item bias* extends this concept to the item level, such as when a particular test stimulus is slanted to unfavorably reflect on one group or their beliefs. Nearly always, test or item bias results in unfairness. This concept moves the definition forward from Cleary's (1968) famous, narrower definition of *statistical bias* in a test as,

> A test is biased for members of a subgroup of the population if, in the prediction of a criterion for which the test was designed, consistent nonzero errors of prediction are made for members of the subgroup. In other words, the test is biased if the criterion score predicted from the common regression line is consistently too high or too low for members of the subgroup. (p. 115)

Cleary's (1968) definition of unequal prediction was useful for many years, but in the modern and broader conception about test differences, it is too limiting. She is closest to our modern description of some DIF detection techniques. The primary importance of Cleary's work is to focus contemporary attention in the field on this important aspect of measurement. Her influence is still felt today, to our benefit.

DIF and Discrimination

While the term *discrimination* in popular speech denotes some unfairness and is often associated with favoritism, intolerance, and even bigotry, when used in psychometric evaluation of tests, it has a wholly different meaning. In psychometric work, the term suggests that the discriminatory feature of a test and its composing items is to make valid and useful distinctions between examinees on the appraised construct. Usually in test work, this is classed as "item discrimination." In fact, in psychometric investigation, discrimination is a positive feature of tests. Reliability is an indicator of the consistency of test discrimination. Clearly, a measure that does not discriminate is unhelpful. Imagine a ruler that makes no distinction between one inch and any other point along its scale. Working from the discrimination feature of tests, then, it is important to appreciate that all DIF detection strategies, to some degree or another, seek to parse useful test discrimination from the undesirable aspect of group differential performance due to something unrelated to the target construct.

To carry out a systematic investigation of such parsing requires that the groups considered in a DIF study be of comparable ability. And, often, many DIF techniques divide each group into smaller subgroups to refine the matching. In summary, then, matching groups by ability on the appraised construct is a paramount feature of all contemporary DIF detection strategies.

Understanding the Term *DIF*

Thus, we see that in the context of studying item performance by group difference, three terms should be considered together: test fairness, test bias, and DIF. As a term, *DIF statistics* describes a growing and evolving collection of statistical techniques useful for detecting systematic differences in performance by subgroups of a population at both test and item levels. There is no one technique or single strategy for investigating DIF; rather, DIF as psychometric nomenclature describes an assemblage of empirical, statistically based techniques targeted at a narrow, but important, part of item investigation. Additionally, DIF neither indicates the direction of detected differences, nor does it connote causation. And, finally, DIF use is primarily confined to statistical and psychometric investigation. Political and policy discussions about group differences should be informed by all three interlocking terms: fairness, test and item bias, and DIF.

Working Vocabulary for This Monograph

Our first charge in this volume—and one that makes it so completely different from the 1983 monograph—is to bring clarity and appreciation to the whole field of studying item influences on differences in test performance across groups. For ease of reading, we use the terms *test* and *mental measure* interchangeably. Additionally, we frequently refer to a test's "items" to mean the more general concept of systematically developed test stimuli. Of course, a test's stimuli can be constructed in many formats: multiple choice, graded responses, other categorical responses, various kinds of constructed responses, and even performances. Particular formats for items (such as dichotomously or polytomously scaled items) are presumed in many DIF detection strategies, and usually, it is obvious from our description; hence, we do not repeat the named format each time. However, when such information is needed for accurate description, we note it.

Also, we use the terms *ability* and *proficiency* interchangeably, although we recognize that they are not synonymous. *Ability* implies latency in the appraised construct, while *proficiency* is more indicative of a skill or a developed talent. However, the distinction, while useful in many psychological contexts, is a distinction without a difference in the context of DIF analyses.

Finally, of course, when referring to educational and psychological tests, we mean only those that are standardized in their administration and have been developed by following precepts that lead to valid and reliable interpretation of their yielded scores. Generally, these follow the guidelines of the *Standards for Educational and Psychological Testing* (American Educational Research Association et al., 1999).

Examples Used in This Monograph

For consistency of approach to the various DIF strategies explained, we illustrate them by using items from a single exam—the College Basic Academic Subjects Examination (College BASE). College BASE is a general achievement test that assesses collegians' knowledge, proficiency, and skills in English, mathematics, science, and social studies and also provides some gauge of their reasoning competence. The focus of College BASE is on determining the degree of mastery or proficiency that has been attained in particular skills and reasoning competencies in a general-education, college curriculum (Osterlind, Sheng, Wang, Beaujean, & Nagel, 2008).

Of course, no identifying information is included so that our statistics may not be traced back to particular items or test forms. Also, all statistics we display are from retired items. Nonetheless, the notion of using items from a single exam gives consistency to our examples, so that the techniques may be reasonably compared and contrasted.

Finally, we used a variety of software to calculate the DIF statistics illustrated, including major programs such as SPSS and SAS and a number of specialized ones such as BILOG-MG, MULTILOG, PARSCALE, and SIBTEST. These are identified throughout the text.

CHAPTER 2. DESCRIPTION OF DIF

Educational and psychological tests are in widespread use in the United States and, now more than ever, all over the world. College admission tests, employment tests, mental health inventories, and other forms of psychological and educational assessments are used to inform policy and practice in a number of social and economic sectors. Test users believe that the test scores are comparable across various groups and that they lead to fair comparisons based on those test scores. However, if the test scores or the test items create or maintain an advantage for one group over another, then the validity of their test-based inferences is threatened (Kane, 2006; Messick, 1989, 1988). Indeed, when a psychological or educational test shows signs of unfairly favoring one demographic group (e.g., men vs. women or blacks vs. whites), it is often assumed to be biased (Camilli, 2006; Cole & Moss, 1989). Often in these circumstances, the test items, themselves, are suspected of functioning differentially across groups—they are exhibiting what measurement experts refer to as "differential item functioning," commonly referred to as DIF (Dorans & Holland, 1993; Holland & Thayer, 1988; Holland & Wainer, 1993).

From a validity perspective, DIF raises concern because its presence suggests that test takers from different demographic groups "have differing probabilities or likelihoods of success on an [test] item, after they have been matched on the psychological characteristic or trait of interest" (Clauser & Mazor, 1998, p. 31). As other researchers have noted, the requirement that performance differences exist, even after matching on the ability of interest, is a central idea, implying, for example, that observed differences in test scores are not, in themselves, evidence of test bias. Indeed, there are times when examinees or respondents from different demographic groups may be expected to differ in ability—for example, when training or learning opportunities are inequitably distributed. In these instances, the result is often termed *item impact* rather than item bias (Camilli, 2006; Camilli & Shepard, 1994; Clauser & Mazor, 1998).

Formal Definition of DIF

In the psychometric literature, a distinction is drawn between "impact" and "measurement bias" or DIF (Camilli, 2006; Camilli & Shepard, 1994; Dorans & Holland, 1993; Millsap & Everson, 1993). Impact refers to consequences of group differences in measured performance on tests or test items. In the areas of education and employment testing, for instance, individuals and groups often differ on the attributes measured by tests; thus, impact is commonly found. Boys typically score higher than girls, for example, on popular measures of mathematics, such as the SAT (SAT Reasoning Test, formerly the Scholastic Aptitude Test and the Scholastic Assessment Test) or the NAEP (the National Assessment of Educational Progress) (Wilder & Powell, 1989).

DIF or measurement bias, in contrast to a test's impact, refers to differences in the way a test item functions across demographic groups that are matched on the attribute measured by the test or the test item (Camilli, 2006; Camilli & Shepard, 1994; Holland & Wainer, 1993; Penfield & Camilli, 2007; Zumbo, 1999). As we noted already, and as others have emphasized too (see Holland & Wainer, 1993), when assessing measurement bias or DIF, it is essential that performance differences be examined only on matched groups to avoid Simpson's paradox (Clifford, 1982; Simpson, 1951). In this paradox, the direction of item impact is inconsistent with the direction of group differences among matched individuals. Again a math example, consider a math item that may be more difficult, overall, for girls, while at the same time it may be less difficult for girls within a group of examinees who have been matched on ability. We often see this finding on tests used in college admissions, for example.

Thus, for purposes of exposition, a formal definition of measurement bias is stated at a general level to give us a preliminary handle on what is truly meant by DIF. Following Millsap and Everson (1993) and Penfield and Camilli (2007), we offer a simple, straightforward example to illustrate the general notion. Here, Y denotes the response to a particular test item, which in itself is determined by the latent construct or ability targeted by the test. The test's latent construct (or ability) is denoted by θ. Following standard notation, Y is the observed indicator of θ. Within this framework, we can express the probability distribution of Y on θ by the functional expression $f(Y)|\theta$. Also, let us suppose that we wish to compare the conditional probability of Y for two groups of examinees, which are referred to as the "focal" and "reference" groups. Statistically, it makes no difference which group is designated as focal and which as reference; however, in the literature the reference group typically comprises individuals whom we suspect the test favors (e.g., the majority group or males), while the focal group is viewed as those individuals who are at risk of being disadvantaged by the test (e.g., minorities or females). Thus, given the functional relationship $f(Y)|\theta$ and the further assumption that the measurement error distributions are identical for both the reference and focal groups, it follows that

$$f(Y|\theta, G = R) = f(Y|\theta, G = F). \qquad (2.1)$$

where G represents the grouping variable, with R corresponding to the reference group and F to the focal group. Equation 2.1, then, represents a situation in which there is an absence of DIF.

To be clear, the absence of DIF is evidenced by a conditional probability distribution of Y that is independent of group membership. For example, suppose we have a test item that is scored dichotomously, where $Y = 1$ indicates a correct response, and $Y = 0$ signifies an incorrect response. In such a situation, the probability of a correct response is identical for individuals belonging to the two groups but having equal status on the θ scale. Clearly, this suggests that the test item is not biased and does not exhibit DIF because members of the reference and focal groups with the same underlying trait or ability level have the same (or essentially the same) chance of indicating a correct response. Thus, we find no evidence of advantage for one group over the other.

This definition of bias flows from the distinction between impact and DIF. The unobserved conditional invariance in Equation 2.1 also constitutes Lord's (1980) definition of lack of item bias, which is often taken as a foundational description of the concept. Indeed, in modern approaches too, Lord's definition forms the basis for methods of DIF detection in applications of IRT (Thissen, Steinberg, & Wainer, 1988). To emphasize, the idea of conditioning on θ in defining item bias is important for distinguishing measurement bias or DIF from ordinary group differences as well as from item impact. For example, it may be true that groups differ in score distributions on Y, or that

$$P(Y|G = g) \neq p(Y). \tag{2.2}$$

There is general consensus in the measurement literature that Equation 2.2 is not sufficient to establish bias as defined above (Ackerman, 1992; Drasgow, 1987; Holland & Thayer, 1988; Lord, 1980; Millsap & Everson, 1993). To the extent that examinee performance depends on θ and that groups differ on θ, Equation 2.2 may indicate bias even if no bias exists. Empirical bias investigations usually proceed on the assumption that group differences on θ are possible or likely.

Now, to carry the case to the next logical step, suppose that the conditional probability of Y is not identical for the reference and focal groups. That is, examinees with the same trait or ability levels, but belonging to different groups, have dissimilar probability distributions on Y. In this case, a dependency is present between group membership and performance on the item once we control for θ (again, assuming equal error distributions). When a test item is scored dichotomously, this conditional dependence suggests that the reference and focal group members at the same level of θ have a different probability of correct response, with the group having the lower conditional probability of correct response being disadvantaged by that particular test item. This line of analysis, then, leads us to conclude that the test item functions differently for the two groups and, consequently, that DIF is extant.

From this discussion, it is apparent that all DIF detection statistics, in one way or another, are concerned with either testing the null hypothesis of no DIF, as described in Equation 2.1, or else they provide a measure of the extent to which Equation 2.1 is not confirmed.

DIF: Uniform or Not

Readers may not find it surprising to learn that attempts at studying DIF have vexed test developers for some time. William Angoff (1993), an early pioneer in the study of test bias at the Educational Testing Service, commented, "It has been reported by test developers that they are often confronted by DIF results that they cannot understand; and no amount of deliberation seems to help explain why some perfectly reasonable items have large DIF values" (p. 19). The ambiguity and confusion experienced by test developers may have something to do with the often unspoken assumption that the test is a unidimensional measure. Indeed, the presence of DIF may indicate that the test is measuring a secondary factor (e.g., test speededness or differing examinee test-taking strategies such as guessing). More often, however, we simply do not know the root causes for DIF.

Regardless, when striving to develop fair and unbiased tests, test developers are often called on to demonstrate if, indeed, a secondary factor is present and, if so, whether it is a deliberate test design characteristic. As we have learned from studies of DIF, often the secondary factor required (or implied) in the test specifications has a different distribution for the reference and focal groups. Thus, to investigate fully if the observed, often inexplicable, DIF is due to the presence of an unintended secondary dimension, test developers often resort to expert review of item content. If, for example, the observed DIF can be linked to otherwise construct irrelevant item content, or some other undesirable item characteristic (method of administration, location in the test, etc.), then the item is thought to be unfair.

To add even more complexity, there are two common types of DIF—uniform and nonuniform. As we have seen, DIF is viewed within a framework of conditional dependence between item performance and examinee group membership. Uniform DIF is the simplest form of DIF, wherein the strength of the conditional dependence remains constant across the underlying θ continuum. That is, the flagged item affords a consistent advantage to the reference group throughout the distribution of θ, for example, when both item characteristic curves (ICCs) have equivalent *a* parameters. Said differently, uniform DIF is present when the probabilities of success on the flagged test item for one group (e.g., the reference group) are consistently higher than the probabilities of success for the focal group over all trait levels (Mellenbergh, 1982). However, there are instances when the nature of this dependency is contingent on where examinees lay on the underlying ability continuum. Thus, nonuniform DIF occurs when the conditional dependence shifts and changes in degree or direction at different points on the θ continuum. As test developers often discover, an item may provide the reference group with a small but negligible advantage at one level of θ and a much larger advantage at higher θ levels. Nonuniform DIF, then, is present when there is an interaction between the trait level (θ) and group membership. More perplexing, test developers sometimes encounter "crossing" nonuniform DIF. This happens when a test item offers an advantage to the reference group at one end of the θ continuum, while the focal group has the relative advantage at the other end of the θ scale.

The difference between uniform and nonuniform DIF can be illustrated by contrasting two item trace lines, as is displayed in Figure 2.1.

As Figure 2.1 suggests, ICCs offer a way to compare the responses of two different groups, for example, the reference and focal groups, to the same test item. A difference between the ICCs suggests that examinees from the two groups, with the identical ability levels, do not have the same probability of success on the test item. Uniform DIF is evident when the ICCs for two groups are different and do not cross. Nonuniform DIF, in contrast, occurs when the ICCs for the two groups differ but cross at some point on the θ scale. Thus, the area between the two ICCs indicates the degree of DIF.

Yet, if the two ICCs cross, a portion of the area can be viewed as positive and some as negative DIF (Camilli & Shepard, 1994). These distinctions are central to understanding and interpreting DIF analyses, and different statistical detection methods may be needed depending on whether we suspect the DIF to be uniform or nonuniform.

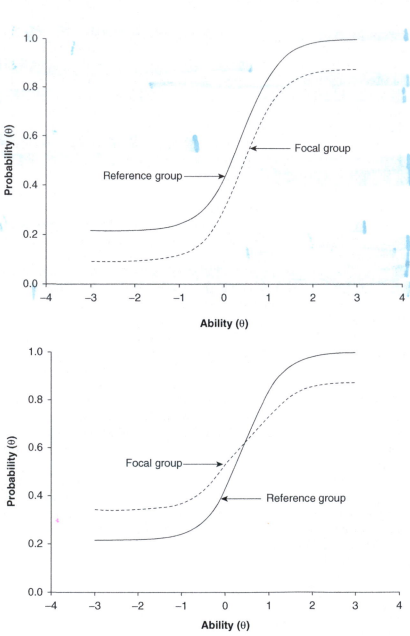

Figure 2.1 Illustrations of Uniform (*top panel*) and Nonuniform (*bottom panel*) DIF.

CHAPTER 3. STATISTICAL FACETS OF DIF

Not Mean (Average) Difference

It is critically important for persons interested in DIF to realize that average (mean or median) score differences between subgroups of a tested population cannot axiomatically be ascribed to DIF, or as even suggesting DIF. Nor do simple group average score differences, in and of themselves, reflect any of the important concepts of DIF, such as unfairness or bias. After all, the essential point of a mental appraisal (i.e., a test) is to reliably unearth a difference in ability or proficiency in the tested construct, and, when properly interpreted, simple mean score differences often do reveal true ability or proficiency differentiation between groups. Of course, analyzing the variance between group score differences is a common statistical strategy to understand the meaning of the difference. Hence, DIF is not an assumption of observed score differences.

Closely related to this idea is the notion that the source of the group differences in DIF exploration is always unrelated to the construct for measurement. That is to say, DIF occurs *because* a factor apart from the test's targeted construct is affecting the performance of one group (i.e., focal group) but not the other (i.e., reference group). For example, if DIF between boys and girls is unearthed in a math item, the DIF occurs because sex or gender is unrelated to the intended measured construct: in this case, math ability or proficiency. But, importantly, we do not know why one sex or the variable gender exhibits the difference in performance; we uncover only that the difference is systematic to the subgroups and that it is mathematically significant. Appreciate, too, that mathematical significance is not identical to statistical significance, as some DIF tests do not validate variance differences in their statistical meaning.

Error in Measurement

When examining DIF in items and tests, it is useful to appreciate the concept of measurement error. Error in measurement is qualitatively different from an "error" in everyday parlance. In our daily lives, we mention that an error has been made, usually with the implication that it could have been avoided had more care been exercised in the first place. In measurement science, however, the idea of error is technical and more complex. It is related to variance in numeracy. *Variance* in educational and psychological measurement derives from probability theory and statistics, and it suggests statistical dispersion of a random variable. Variance is mathematically defined as the square of the standard deviation. In a properly derived sample, error exists when a given number is not as *expected* (i.e., the mean). In the aggregate of all numbers in a sample, there is variance. The deviation of a number in the variance is termed *error*. Similarly, reliability is detecting error in a given measurement process, and it is indexed by any of several values. DIF is itself a measure of error, too. Furthermore, measurement error is categorized in two ways: random or systematic. Osterlind (2006) describes the differences between the kinds of error.

> It is useful to realize that there are many kinds of error, or stated more precisely, *sources of error*. Generally, sources of error are cataloged as either *random* or *systematic*. Random error is the difference between an individual's true score and observed score, whereas systematic error comprises consistent differences between groups that are unrelated to the construct or the proficiency being assessed. The differentiating aspect of these two kinds of measurement error is the target: Random error applies to an individual, whereas systematic error applies to group responses. (p. 59)

DIF methods have been developed largely to detect this latter source of error. However, after more than 30 years of research on item bias and DIF, it has become apparent that the sources of DIF are often not as systematic as first believed. Nor are they obvious or easily uncovered. For example, sometimes we find DIF in only a small portion (a subpopulation) of the focal group and not in the entire focal group. As we have learned, the sources of DIF can be rather subtle at times.

Differences Are Systematic

As mentioned above, another important consideration about DIF is that the score differences to be investigated must be, in some way, *systematic*. That is, the discrepancy between subgroups must affect all or nearly all persons in the same, and predictable, manner. Most often, in DIF investigation, the focal group is systematically disadvantaged in responding to the test item when compared with an appropriate reference group. This notion captures the effect of test- and item bias. And, following this notion, DIF does not apply to an individual's performance on a single test item. It is always understood to apply to a group phenomenon.

Matching on Ability or Proficiency

From this realization, it is apparent that a critically important part of all procedures of DIF investigation is to match examinees by ability or proficiency on the appraised construct. The matching is usually done by total test score. In most DIF methods, the total test score is taken as a proxy for an examinee's ability or proficiency. Thus, examinees of similar ability or proficiency are also compared and contrasted by their performance on a given test item.

Also, it is assumed that the subgroups for comparison are important to the larger examinee population, or the universe of examinees. That is, the reference and focal subgroups in a DIF investigation must be connected to some appropriate purpose. For instance, it is common to look into DIF between the sexes or between racial categories or persons of various ethnic heritages. Each of these subgroups is germane to many research and psychometric investigations, and they are sensible subgroups. However, it is nonsense to examine DIF between, say, persons of different handedness (left-handed vs. right-handed) or between differences in cranium sizes.

Conditioning Criterion: Internal Versus External

As has been emphasized, DIF and related issues assume meaning only when examinees of plausibly equivalent ability are contrasted. Therefore, determining even rough equanimity is worth careful attention, lest the results become tenuous.

One early consideration is whether the matching criterion should be internal or external to the test in which the DIF analysis is made. An external criterion can be another test or other assessment that is meaningfully related to the appraised focus of the target test. For example, using a test of general intelligence may be considered for external criterion when the target test is of school- or knowledge-based achievement.

An external criterion for matching abilities or proficiencies of the reference and focal groups can be useful because such a criterion is likely to be less contaminated by factors in the target test that are intrinsically unrelated to DIF, such as test length or considerations of the test administration environment. However, employing an external criterion for matching can be fraught with dangers, too. There are a few important principles to follow in this regard. First, the external criterion must be itself meritorious, determined only after careful evaluation of its reliability and its validity in the present context. Second, and related to internal validity, the external criterion must be appropriate for this use. For instance, one should not employ an instrument of personality appraisal as external criterion for DIF evaluation of an aptitude test. And, other conditions may be necessary for evaluation in a given DIF research context. For instance, the DIF detection methods used may influence a decision about using an external criterion. Hambleton and Bollward (1990) and colleagues studied

DIF comparisons with both internal and external criteria and reported that with Mantel-Haenszel (M-H) procedures, the results for DIF item identification were similar. However, their study was limited in scope. Unfortunately, there is a dearth of research in this important area, and investigators are cautioned to proceed carefully and thoughtfully when using an external criterion for matching in DIF analyses.

In many (perhaps most) situations, a suitable external criterion is not available, making an internal criterion the only way to proceed. The logical choice here is to use total test score as the criterion. Implicitly, the total test score will most closely reflect relevant attributes for DIF investigation; so it is often a reasonable means for matching. To this end, the test's reliability should be known and considered appropriately beforehand. Mostly, however, researchers should have a clear understanding of the matching criterion. Using total test score simply because it is available is often inappropriate for thoughtful DIF investigation.

Purification of Data

A common question that arises from using an internal criterion concerns whether to include a particular suspect test item or task as a contributor to the criterion or to exclude it. Excluding the item from the matching criterion (e.g., total test score) is a process termed *purification*. The choice of whether to purify the test prior to analysis is not an easy one because at matching no DIF has yet been detected and hence excluding the item may be irrational. Yet, when DIF is suspected for a given item, it seems logical to purify the test. One solution to this dilemma is to conduct preliminary DIF analyses, then omit suspected items and recalculate the total score. An appealing feature of purification is that it is easy to do and can be used with any of the DIF statistics, including IRT-based ones. Clauser and Mazor (1998) suggest that this practice does not increase the Type I error rate. And, Stout (1995) incorporates this as an option with SIBTEST (Simultaneous Item Bias Test), a DIF detection program that implements a nonparametric statistical method (see Shealy & Stout, 1993) discussed later. However, purification can also be addressed from a more sophisticated perspective.

Two more thorough purification methods are an iterative purification procedure and a two-step purification procedure. Both of these routes for purification address power and misidentification with false positives. Originally introduced by Birnbaum (1968) on his seminal chapter on latent trait models in Lord and Novick's (1968) important *Statistical Theories of Mental Test Scores*. Later work on the iterative procedures was contributed by Shepard, Camilli, and Averil (1981) and especially Shealy and Stout

(1993). In the iterative purification procedure, one identifies the highest significant item value for the items on a test. Usually, this is done by the M-H DIF method. Next, the DIF item is omitted from consideration, while test statistics are again computed. If the original DIF-identified item is still significant, then the next highest (i.e., significant) item is also eliminated. Item statistics are once again computed. This process continues iteratively until a significance criterion is reached or a predetermined number of iterations are arrived at. As an alternative, instead of eliminating a single item, two (those with the highest significance values) are removed. This causes the iterations to terminate more quickly.

The two-step purification procedure was originally proposed by Holland and Thayer (1988). In the first step of this procedure, DIF statistics (usually by M-H, per usual) are calculated. When the critical value for significance is obtained (regardless of whether it is $\alpha = .05$ or $\alpha = .01$, usual criteria), the item is eliminated. As a second step, the test statistics are recomputed using the same DIF methodology. Researchers investigating these procedures (see Kwak, Davenport, & Davison, 1998) report that power in identification, and fewer false positives are misidentified.

CHAPTER 4. IMPORTANT CONSIDERATIONS

There are a number of useful and important considerations in DIF investigation. We identify several of them here, although others probably exist in particular circumstances. Researchers should be mindful of these issues, as heeding them will aid in the interpretation of DIF results.

DIF: Statistics Versus Reasoned Judgment

First and possibly even foremost when investigating DIF in mental measures, the researcher should recognize that analyzing test items is an exercise requiring not only psychometric and statistical skill but also good judgment—even wisdom. Such skill and judgment are needed even when the item's analysis is relatively straightforward, as, for instance, when examining the difficulty and the discriminating power of an item. But the measurement expert's skills and judgment are called into play even more when exploring DIF between subgroups of a population. This is so because interpreting findings of a DIF study is not always straightforward. Commonly, different results are obtained when different DIF detection strategies are used, and just as often items that exhibit statistical DIF, on inspection, display no obvious reason for the disparity in performance, as, for example, when DIF is indicated in a simple arithmetic computation problem. Hence, we urge researchers, and others doing DIF work, to be extra careful in their work, and use not only their full range of statistical and measurement expertise but also reasoned judgment with a healthy dose of common sense. Bringing a sagacious attitude to the study of DIF will, no doubt, aid in gaining a proper perspective on the work.

This point can be brought into play for persons working with DIF when they recognize that most DIF studies unearth some evidence of DIF in a particular test or mental measure. The sophisticated researcher knows that it cannot be concluded from this realization that tests are commonly biased or unfair or will have adverse impact. DIF is a statistical strategy with assumptions and an inherent uncertainty. As with all statistical procedures, false positives can occur. Studying DIF is an inexact science, albeit still useful when its results are properly interpreted in a knowing context.

Statistical Bias Is Not Unfairness

Also, when conducting a DIF investigation, it is appropriate and useful to appreciate that psychometric bias is not the same as statistical bias. In statistical work, "bias" is the difference between the expected value and the true value of the parameter being estimated. As is well known, in statistics, properties of unbiased estimators are useful for research generalizations. In DIF work, however, bias occurs when significant differences on item performance occur systematically for examinees of similar ability or proficiency.

Whole Test Versus Individual Items

When a researcher sets about studying DIF, a number of practical questions arise. An early sensible question often asked is whether to study DIF in an entire test just after isolating particular items, making a smaller set of them for analysis. We recommend that the researcher study the entire set of items in a test simultaneously. The reason for our recommendation is that DIF is a phenomenon that cannot be readily recognized by eyeballing test items; hence, knowing which items from among a set of them to analyze prior to analysis is dubious. And, test constructors place items together for the feature of the collective strength to reliably represent a construct. The number of items necessary for DIF work varies considerably from construct to construct, as well as for proper scaling and other psychometric reasons. Generally, a test length of about 20 items is sufficient for DIF investigation.

Another commonly asked practical question concerns the number of examinees necessary for DIF research. When examinees are selected for the reference and focal groups based on their race or ethnic heritage, unequal sample sizes often result, and researchers should be especially mindful of the relative size for each sample. Of course, researchers should examine the size and shape of the relative groups, examining their normality, linearity, and homoscedasticity (homogeneity of variance). The overarching issue here is for reliable sampling, a subject outside the scope of this monograph. Nonetheless, it is useful to bear in mind that the hypotheses for comparisons in DIF are of two independent groups (reference and focal) or samples. Tests for the independence of samples may provide useful information about the size needed for a reliable DIF study. The independent group t test is called on for these questions. Alternatively, when the assumption of normality or equality of variance is not met, a nonparametric test such as the U statistics for the Mann-Whitney test can be used to gain insight.

Number: Items and Sample

In DIF investigation, at least three numerical sizes need consideration, including (1) the number of examinees in each of the reference and focal groups, (2) the number of items within a test for DIF investigation, and (3) the length of the test from which the items are to be sampled. Each numerical size has its own set of issues for the researcher to reflect on. The overarching issues are determining a size that is sufficient for reliable conclusion by the statistics employed and the generalizing capacity of the sample to other groups or a population.

The third issue may be the simplest to consider, so we address it first. Zumbo (1999) recommends that a test length of at least 20 items as a minimum be used. His primary thought is that the overall score should be meaningful and useful when employed as a matching criterion. Hence, the test's length is important. Obviously, a test with less than desirable validity characteristics is not appropriate as a gauge of the overarching construct. So the researcher should examine a test's internal characteristics as well as the intent of the appraised construct. Reliability and validity are the focus here. A test designed to appraise a narrowly focused construct will generally require fewer items for reliable score interpretation than does a test that aims to measure a more obtuse construct. Osterlind (2006) offers a useful discussion of test evaluation in this regard.

The next numerical issue is to determine the number of items within a test that will be subject to DIF investigation. Here, there is no rule of thumb, as this number must be determined anew in each DIF study. Simply including all items in an investigation is sometimes appropriate, but at other times it is not. A proper route for the researcher to follow is to first determine the reason and scope for the overall DIF investigation. Then, using this information, the researcher makes an informed judgment about the number of items, as well as which of them will fulfill the study's purpose.

The final numerical consideration is to determine the number of examinees to be included in the reference and focal groups. In most studies, both theoretical and practical considerations interplay. Obviously, usually known is the number of subjects available within each group. When the groups are based on sex, gender, or racial identification (as many DIF studies are), this number is often immediately at hand. But it may not be sufficiently large for meaningful statistical power. Also, the groups may be disproportionate in size, occasionally massively so. Sometimes combining ethnic groups into a single category and then using dummy coding for "majority" and "nonmajority" can be done. Particularly, the researcher should be mindful to not have massively disproportionate numbers between the reference and focal groups, lest power in the statistics be compromised.

However, the sample size considerations do not end there. The particular statistics often have sample requirements of their own. For example, an analysis using the chi-square may require fewer subjects than one based on IRT. Also significant, the distributional characteristics of the sample should be explored. Most statistics presume normality, linearity, and homo-scedesticity in the sample for their proper interpretation. And, some other statistics have special issues, such as in a regression-based procedure, the sample should be examined for leveraged values as well as other outliers. A useful source for determining sample size for generalizing is Williams's (1978) sampling primer cleverly titled *A Sampler on Sampling*.

A Sensible Perspective

Finally, it is important to view DIF investigations from a sensible perspective. Commonly, DIF is detected for some number of items in a test, especially when many items are considered in a single study. But, when the researcher scrutinizes the identified test item(s), there may be no obvious reason for the discrepancy. For instance, a simple arithmetic problem may show DIF between girls and boys. Here, the researcher's skill, experience, and common sense must come into play. Sometimes, for reasons unknown, calculations of a DIF detection strategy may suggest DIF, where none truly exists. And, importantly, the researcher must realize that a test should not be summarily dismissed by the detection of some DIF in some items. If that were the case, nearly every instrument ever devised would be discarded, and we know through numerous other psychometric evaluations and by experience that this is unwarranted. We live in an imperfect world.

CHAPTER 5. HISTORY OF TEST BIAS AND DIF

DIF and issues of test bias, though statistical and quantitative, are best understood when grounded in the larger contemporary social and legal context of test fairness and equal opportunity. To provide that context, a number of important historical, social, and legal concepts are presented and discussed briefly in this section.

Little attention was given to issues of test fairness and item bias until the 1960s. In the United States, the historic Civil Rights Act of 1964 was enacted and signed into law by President Lyndon Johnson. This new law ushered in what is now referred to as the era of civil rights, and steps toward equality and equal opportunity began to influence testing practices in the education and employment sectors of American society. The 1964 Civil Rights Act is regularly updated and reauthorized by Congress. The sweeping changes brought about by the act focused measurement professionals' attention on the issue of using tests in employment and educational contexts where adverse impact may result. *Adverse impact* is a legal term referring to prima facie evidence in support of claims of unlawful discrimination. Writing in the early 1980s, Berk (1982), the editor of a seminal collection of papers outlining novel statistical methods to detect item bias, noted, "In the late 1960s and early 1970s psychometricians hastened to provide definitions of bias in terms of objective criteria, to develop rigorous and precise methods for studying bias, and to consider empirical investigations of test bias" (p. 1).

Striking a similar note, Nancy Cole (1993), a former president of the Educational Testing Service, underscored the influence of the civil rights era on test fairness when she wrote that "test and item bias concerns in their modern form grew out of this era, were responses to it, were influenced by it, and took their role as a standard part of the [testing] enterprise because of it" (p. 25).

Thus, in response to social change, and as a practical operational matter, reviewing a test for fairness became a major activity for test developers and users alike.

During the post–civil rights period, we find test publishers implementing fairness reviews and developing empirical measures to help identify items that may be unfair to one group or another. Today, test fairness reviews are central to the test design and development process of most professional testing groups and organizations (Zieky, 2006).

Standards for Test Fairness

Recognizing the growing importance of psychological and educational testing and their central roles in modern, civil society, three prominent professional organizations—the American Educational Research Association, the American Psychological Association, and the National Council on Measurement in Education—worked collaboratively to develop the current version of the *Standards for Educational and Psychological Testing* (American Educational Research Association et al., 1999). These jointly developed standards evolved over time—the current edition is the fourth iteration of this publication—and grew out of earlier work done by the three professional organizations that dates back to the mid-1950s, even predating the civil rights era. As such, the 1999 *Standards* reflect the professional measurement community's attempt to address both the social and the technical issues of test fairness.

Commenting on the role and importance of the 1999 *Standards*, Camilli (2006) cites the following definition of test fairness:

Fairness in testing refers to perspectives on the ways that scores from tests or items are interpreted in the process of evaluating test takers for a selection or classification decision. Fairness in testing is closely related to test validity, and the evaluation of fairness requires a broad range of evidence that includes empirical data, but may also involve legal, ethical, political, philosophical, and economic reasoning. (p. 225)

When addressing fairness in testing, the 1999 *Standards* (American Psychological Association et al., 1999) note that, indeed, there is broad consensus that tests ought to be free from bias; and they defined bias as

[arising] when deficiencies in a test itself or the manner in which it is used result in different meanings for scores earned by members of different identifiable subgroups. When evidence of such deficiencies is found at the level of item response patterns for members of different groups, the terms item bias or differential item functioning (DIF) are often used. . . . There is general consensus that consideration of bias is critical to sound testing practice. (p. 74)

Holland and Thayer (1988) make a similar point in an important chapter describing the Mantel-Haenszel DIF procedure (Mantel & Haenszel, 1959). When elaborating on its use as an empirical DIF method, Holland and Thayer (1988) note that

the performance of two groups may be compared in terms of a test item, a total test score, or prediction regarding success on a criterion. The focal group (or group F), which is sometimes called the protected group, is of primary interest. This group is to be compared to a second group, labeled the reference or base group (or group R). The previous terminology of minority and majority groups is no longer used. (p. 130)

Thus, in a typical DIF analysis, the first step is to define the reference and focal groups. Then one can use statistical methods to estimate the differences between the two groups. It is important, both legally and from a measurement perspective, to keep in mind that differential group performance may be the result of real, bona fide educational and (or) psychological differences between groups.

Again, as the 1999 *Standards* make clear, test fairness does not imply equal test scores or equal classification outcomes. Within this framework, fairness reviews have to be designed and conducted to determine empirically, where possible, whether the observed group differences are the result of influences beyond the scope of the test or, perhaps, to construct irrelevant test features. To provide guidance to the professions, the 1999 *Standards* offer the following definition of statistical bias when examining group performance differences at the item level:

> Differential item functioning exists when examinees of equal ability differ, on average, according to their group membership in their responses to a particular item. (p. 81)

A comprehensive discussion of the 1999 *Standards* is beyond the scope of this book and would take us far afield from the focus of this monograph. A recent thorough treatment of the 1999 *Standards* and how they relate to the broader issues of test fairness and test bias can be found in Camilli (2006).

Looking back, we see that the development of statistical methods for identifying potentially biased test items began in earnest in the late 1970s. However, it was nearly a decade later—in the mid- to late 1980s—that a general, workable statistical framework ultimately emerged that would serve as the foundation for the analysis of item bias on a broad scale. This framework, commonly referred to today as "DIF statistics," was introduced in a series of papers by Paul Holland and his colleagues at the Educational Testing Service (see Holland, 1985; Holland & Thayer, 1988). In the more than 20 years since Holland and Thayer's series, the DIF framework has produced an enormous wave of research and development to detect test item bias. DIF methods have been integrated into test validity studies and, as we noted earlier, have been incorporated into the 1999 *Standards*—directly in Standard 7.3. In addition, as Penfield and Camilli (2007) point out, DIF statistics have now spread to other, related fields in psychology and the health sciences that rely on standardized measures of psychological constructs (see Bolt, 2002; Dodeen & Johanson, 2003; Gelin, Carelton, Smith, & Zumbo, 2004; Lange, Thalbourne, Houran, & Lester, 2002). In these areas outside of educational testing, DIF methods aid researchers in thinking more broadly about the validity issues inherent in their efforts to assess between-group differences on traits measured with constructed measures.

CHAPTER 6. QUICK-BUT-INCOMPLETE METHODS

Sometimes, it is useful to garner information about discrepancies in item performance between groups prior to formal DIF investigation. A simple, early look can often be a purposeful rough guide to more thorough—and precise—DIF exploration. These initial examinations employ only simple statistics and uncomplicated investigative strategies. That is their strength. We call these item exploration schemes "quick-but-incomplete methods" because that is just what they are: While they provide useful rough guides, they do not develop information of sufficient accuracy or thoroughness to imply DIF. Hence, at the outset, we caution that such a precursory look is neither conclusive of true differences, nor do results of these simplistic methods provide direct evidence for DIF. Nonetheless, with appropriate skepticism, such early looks can yield valuable suggestions about group performance differences. An additional short-coming of these quick-but-incomplete methods is that none of them can detect discrepancies between subgroups that are not uniform across all levels of the ability range. In DIF terminology, then, these strategies can suggest only investigation into uniform DIF. They do not provide information indicative of nonuniform DIF.

Ordinal Ranking of Items

The first of these quick-but-incomplete methods is to compare ordinal rankings of suspect items for the two groups (reference and focal). Here, items' p values are calculated for each group without regard to ability (or proficiency) level distinctions. These p values are then ranked in an ordinal fashion and placed in a comparison table where differences between the groups can be scrutinized for contrasts. Table 6.1 illustrates the procedure.

In the table, proportion passing rates (i.e., p values) for five items are displayed. These p values are ranked by their performance for each group and set in columns for easy comparison. As seen in the table, Item 2 is the highest ranking (first ordinal value) for both groups, thereby suggesting little distinction in performance. However, note that Item 4 does show an overall group discrepancy between the p value rankings. Item 4 exhibits the second highest p value for the reference group but only the fifth highest value for the focal group. By this preliminary look, then, this item warrants further investigation into group differences. Again, notice particularly for this method that between-group abilities (or proficiencies)

Table 6.1   Rank Order of Item Difficulties for Two Groups

	Reference Group		Focal Group	
Item	Rank	p-Value	Rank	p-Value
1	3rd	.64	2nd	.62
2	1st	.93	1st	.81
3	4th	.55	3rd	.51
4	2nd	.71	5th	.19
5	5th	.37	4th	.28

are not matched, and thus, caution is advised against making DIF interpretations from this sparse information. Nevertheless, this method is illustrated because it presents group contrasts, and the method is quick and simple.

Ability Group Methods

An improvement on the ordinal-ranking method—but still not sufficient to evidence full DIF interpretations—can be gained by dividing each group by overall ability and then comparing the ability levels. Many classical item analysis programs can conveniently perform the necessary calculations, including the popular TESTFACT (Wood et al., 2003). We use another program called MERMAC to illustrate this procedure. In this program, the performance for each group is again calculated independently; however, the ability distribution for each group is divided into fractiles, in this case, fifths. A display for each group is given in Figure 6.1. The top panel shows performance values for the reference group, and the bottom panel presents parallel numbers for the focal group. The raw number of responses for each correct response (indicated by the parentheses around the D option) and the distractor is given, along with the p value (labeled DIFF) and the point biserial correlation coefficient (labeled RPBIS).

From the two panel displays in Figure 6.1, it is easy to recognize that overall performance on the item is discrepant: p values equal .73 and .06, respectively, for the reference and focal groups. Also apparent in Figure 6.1 is the fact that this difference is nearly uniform across all ability levels. A strength of this method is that the display reveals where the distinction between the group occurs; here, the focal group is overwhelmingly drawn

Reference Group

```
Matrix of Responses by Fifths for Question 91
         D Is Correct Response                    Percent of Correct Response by Fifths for Question 91
        A     B     C    (D)    E   OMIT
5th     0     8    15   135     0     0    5th +                                              *
4th     2    14    23   114     0     0    4th +                                        *
3rd     1     8    26   130     0     0    3rd +                                          *
2nd     1    11    32   107     0     1    2nd +                                     *
1st     5    24    37    93     0     5    1st +                             *
                                           +----+----+----+----+----+----+----+----+----+----+
DIFF  0.01  0.08  0.17 (0.73) 0.00  0.01   0   10   20   30   40   50   60   70   80   90  100
RPBI -0.09 -0.11 -0.15 (0.24) 0.00 -0.15
```

Focal Group

```
Matrix of Responses by Fifths for Question 91
         D Is Correct Response                    Percent of Correct Response by Fifths for Question 91
        A     B     C    (D)    E   OMIT
5th     4   116    22    10     0     0    5th +  *
4th     6   107    28    11     0     0    4th +  *
3rd     5   110    26    11     0     0    3rd +  *
2nd     7   121    26     4     0     0    2nd +*
1st    16   106    25     8     0     0    1st +  *
                                           +----+----+----+----+----+----+----+----+----+----+
DIFF  0.05  0.73  0.17 (0.06) 0.00  0.00   0   10   20   30   40   50   60   70   80   90  100
RPBI -0.12  0.05  0.00 (0.02) 0.00  0.00
```

Figure 6.1   Illustration of Classical Item Analyses by Ability Group for Two Groups on the Same Item

to distractor B (the incorrect response option). Thus, researchers are advised to examine the item and to search for reasons why the focal group may be attracted to the particular distractor. Also, researchers need to be mindful that the fractile groups, although used as proxy ability groupings, are calculated independently and, hence, are not matched on ability, a major shortcoming for DIF investigation.

To obviate the troubling circumstance of comparing nonmatched ability groups, it is necessary to calculate the matching first and then run the item analysis. Matching the groups by ability before comparisons—a necessary condition for justifiable DIF work—moves the comparison procedures closer to the M-H method. M-H procedures are suitable for serious DIF investigation, and they are described in the following section.

Outdated ANOVA Methods

Analyzing variance ratios by ANOVA is mentioned here only because it is still widely extant in the literature, and our experience suggests that many do not yet realize that it is out of date. While early investigators of DIF (done at a time when the phenomenon was generally labeled as *item bias*) (e.g., Berk, 1982; Jensen, 1980) suggested simple ANOVA as a useful detection strategy, this procedure has now been largely discarded because it simply analyzes between-group variance ratios for the entire sample and does not match examinees on ability or proficiency, a necessary condition for DIF. Shortcomings of ANOVA methods are addressed specifically with SIBTEST, a procedure discussed later. Some recent research, however, employs ANOVA in combination with IRT-based scaling techniques with some success (Whitmore & Schumacker, 1999), but more work in this area is required before the procedure can be recommended again.

CHAPTER 7. MANTEL-HAENSZEL PROCEDURE

As we have seen, in early DIF (and initially "item bias") investigations, researchers sought ways to contrast the distributions of the reference of focal groups through ANOVA and other distributional statistics, albeit some of these attempts were problematic from the outset and ultimately proved unsuccessful. Another obvious means for this kind of comparison was to employ the chi-square test to look for significance. However, a simple chi-square statistic is by itself inappropriate for such comparisons since proportions cannot be used with the statistical test directly. Additionally, the chi-square test is notoriously unreliable with small frequencies, a common circumstance in DIF group selection. And, finally, when the chi-square is employed in DIF work with multiple degrees of freedom, it lacks adequate power to meaningfully evaluate specific alternatives to null DIF hypotheses (see Holland & Thayer, 1988). For these reasons, then, we do not recommend ordinary chi-square methods.

However, two medical researchers working in the 1950s—the biostatistician Nathan Mantel and the epidemiologist William Haenszel—realizing the inherent difficulties of the chi-square test, developed a summary chi-square procedure tailored for stratified samples (Mantel & Haenszel, 1959). They sought to take advantage of the chi-square test's strength as a measure of linear association between the row and column variables in a cross-tabulation, a clearly useful display of group comparisons. The work of Mantel and Haenszel was to develop a variation of Cochran's statistic with small-sample corrections for continuity and variance inflation. More than two decades later, their modified chi-square procedure was taken up by Holland (1985), who proposed it as a practical approach to detecting DIF. As a consequence of the work by Holland (1985) and Holland and Thayer (1988), this DIF methodology is named after Mantel and Haenszel as the "Mantel-Haenszel procedure" (M-H) and is today possibly the most commonly used DIF detection strategy.

In this section, we discuss M-H primarily as applied to items that are scored as a dichotomy (i.e., correct vs. incorrect) since this is the most frequent case; however, the M-H method has been extended for detecting DIF in polytomous items. Such use of DIF is discussed below in a devoted section.

Chi-Square Contingency Table

The M-H procedure is based on a chi-square distribution but employs a variant of the usual chi-square (with a contingency table) called the *full chi-square*. With the full chi-square, the variable of interest (i.e., test items) is theoretically conceived as representing a psychological continuum from none at all to full, much as is done in a full-information factor analysis with tetrachoric correlations. With a statistical adjustment, it can be usefully applied to group comparisons in DIF work.

Procedurally, in M-H, the reference and focal groups are divided into ability or proficiency strata based on their overall test score, thus setting into operation the matched-groups condition for DIF evaluation. Usually, four or five ability levels are developed. Next, for each ability level, a 2×2 chi-square contingency table is prepared. In the tables, frequency counts of correct and incorrect responses for each group at each ability level are presented, as illustrated in Figure 7.1. Realize that Figure 7.1 presents data for just a single ability level, and three or four parallel tables at other ability strata are developed, making it more fully a $2 \times 2 \times k$ chi-square contingency table, where k indicates the number of groups.

The general form of M-H data organization is given in Figure 7.2.

Item 23; Ability Level 2			
	Correct	Incorrect	TOTALS
Reference *(R)*	164	97	261
Focal *(F)*	102	144	246
Totals	266	241	507

Figure 7.1 Mantel-Haenszel Chi-Square Table for One Item at One Ability Level

Item i; Ability Level j			
	1	0	
Reference *(R)*	a_i	b_i	$N_{R,} = a_i + c_i$
Focal *(F)*	c_i	d_i	$N_{F,} = b_i + d_i$
Totals	$N_{1,}$	$N_{0,}$	
	$N_{1,} = a_i + c_i$	$N_{0,} = b_i + d_i$	$N_{T,} = a_i + b_i + c_i + d_i$

Figure 7.2 General Form of Mantel-Haenszel Chi-Square Table for One Item at One Ability Level

The statistical hypothesis for data arranged as shown in Figure 7.2 is, of course, conditional independence of group membership. However, this hypothesis requires that the observed data in the table be a sampling model. Hence, the values of the marginals (N_{R_i} and N_{F_i}), where R is the referral group and F is the focal group for item i at ability j and N is the total number, are treated as population parameters where the observed values are random samples of n_{R_i} and n_{F_i}, and are shown in the table as a_i, b_i, c_i, and d_i.

M-H Odds Ratio

M-H calculations begin as an odds ratio of p/q, where p represents the odds of a correct response to the item and $q = 1 - p$, in the usual fashion. In M-H, this odds ratio is typically denoted by α_{MH}, and it expresses a linear association between the row and column variables in the table. Different authors follow different formulas to calculate the odds ratio, but working from a contingency table such as the one given in Figure 6.1, the odds ratio may be calculated as shown in Equation 7.1 below:

$$\alpha_i = \frac{p_{r_i}/q_{r_i}}{p_{f_i}/q_{f_i}} = \frac{\frac{a_i/(a_i+b_i)}{b_i/(a_i+b_i)}}{\frac{c_i/(c_i+d_i)}{d_i/(c_i+d_i)}} = \frac{a_i/b_i}{c_i/d_i} = \frac{a_i d_i}{b_i c_i}, \tag{7.1}$$

where p_{r_i} is the proportion of the reference group (r) in the score interval i who answered the item correctly.

q_{r_i} is the proportion of the reference group (r) in the score interval i who answered incorrectly (i.e., $q_{r_i} = 1 - p_{r_i}$), and similarly for the focal group (i.e., p_{f_i} and q_{f_i}).

If there is no difference between the groups, then the odds ratio is at 1 (i.e., $\alpha_i = 1$), indicating equilibrium between the reference and focal groups and interpreted as no DIF. However, when $\alpha_i > 1$, the reference group performs significantly better on the item than the focal group, at least for that ability strata. Conversely, for $\alpha_i < 1$, the focal group has significantly outperformed the reference group at the ability level.

More precisely, α_i is an index estimating the weighted average score in which the odds that a person in the reference group endorses the correct choice for the item exceed the parallel odds for someone in the focal group. In essence, this is a t test distributed on 1 df with the customary significance criterion level of $p < .05$.

Also, α_i is used to represent a population estimate; and to more accurately reflect this across-groups representation, it is noted as $\hat{\alpha}_{MH}$, a common odds ratio. This statistic can be estimated for the matched groups in all strata, as shown in Equation 7.2.

$$\hat{\alpha}_{\text{MH}} = \frac{\sum_i p_{r_i} q_{f_i} N_{r_i} \frac{N_{f_i}}{N_i}}{\sum_i q_{r_i} p_{r_i} N_{r_i} \frac{N_{f_i}}{N_i}} = \frac{\sum_i \frac{a_i d_i}{N_i}}{\sum_i \frac{b_i c_i}{N_i}}. \tag{7.2}$$

While this value represents the population of DIF for a given item, the value of $\hat{\alpha}_{\text{MH}}$ is difficult to interpret, and typically it is transformed to the more convenient log scale. The transformation is given in Equation 7.3, and the resultant index is noted as $\text{MH}_{D-\text{DIF}}$.

$$\text{MH}_{D-\text{DIF}} = -2.35\ln(\hat{\alpha}_{\text{MH}}). \tag{7.3}$$

This new scale references the center of the index around zero, so that $\text{MH}_{D-\text{DIF}} = 0$, where 0 is interpreted as the absence of any DIF, as described above. Also note the minus sign, as this reverses the interpretation so that when $\text{MH}_{D-\text{DIF}}$ is positive, the item favors the focal group, and when it is negative, the item favors the reference group.

Figure 7.3 displays commonly reported M-H statistics. This is an SPSS, v. 16 output (SPSS, 2008), although many other programs also calculate M-H statistics, including, SAS, Stata, R, and Systat.

Both the real-number value and transformed log values for $\hat{\alpha}_{\text{MH}}$ are given. The number of examinees in this example is relatively large; however, the yielded values for smaller samples are comparable. As seen in the figure, Item 25 exhibits DIF between the gender groups (males are the reference group, and females are the focal group), while Item 26 does not. This is shown by the significance of the difference from a hypothesized zero difference.

Thus, as can be seen in this example, the M-H is a relatively straightforward procedure that can be used in many testing analyses.

Crosstab for Gender by Q25				
Count		Gender		
		male	female	Total
rq25	0	115	132	247
	1	145	105	250
	Total	260	237	497

Crosstab for Gender by Q26				
Count		Gender		
		male	female	Total
rq26	0	108	90	198
	1	152	147	299
	Total	260	237	497

Tests of Conditional Independence					
	Chi-Squared		df	Asymp.Sig.(2-sided)	
	Q25	Q26		Q25	Q26
Cochran's	6.520	0.657	1	0.011	0.418
Mantel-Haenszel	6.057	0.516	1	0.014	0.473

(Continued)

(Continued)

Mantel-Haenszel Common Odds Ratio Estimate					
				Q25	Q26
Estimate				0.631	1.161
ln(Estimate) Std. Error of ln(Estimate)				−0.461 0.181	0.149 0.184
Asymp. Sig. (2-sided)				0.011	0.418
Asymp. 95% Confidence Interval	Common Odds Ratio	Lower Bound		0.443	0.810
		Upper Bound		0.899	1.664
	ln (Common Odds Ratio)	Lower Bound		−0.815	−0.211
		Upper Bound		−0.106	0.509
The Mantel-Haenszel common odds ratio estimate is asymptotically normally distributed under the common odds ratio of 1.000 assumption, as is the natural log of the estimate.					

Figure 7.3   SPSS Output for M-H

CHAPTER 8. NONPARAMETRIC METHODS

DIF methods that do not rely on population (i.e., probability distribution) assumptions provide a wholly different perspective on the investigation of aberrant functioning in items. These nonparametric approaches are not based on any statistical or probability model, making them suitable to consider DIF investigation across tests. This perspective is their appeal, for by them DIF is construed as a dimensional issue in assessment and not a feature of a particular test. Several methods are available for nonparametric investigation of DIF.

DIF With SIBTEST

As DIF work moves increasingly into realms of test use and applicability of test scores for decision making, there is a corresponding increase in attention to the impact of difference functioning, bias, and unfairness. Shealy and Stout (1993) particularized this concern into dimensionality examination with their SIBTEST, a strategy for DIF that also corrects the unstandardized M-H with a linear regression correction. Shealy and Stout define "SIB" in the title as "simultaneous item bias" (p. 159). As a "simultaneous" procedure it can detect either DIF at the item level or bias as a test characteristic. In the method, the means on a given item are adjusted to correct for differences in the distributions of ability for the reference and focal groups using a regression correction. The aim of this approach is to more accurately match the reference and focal groups than is done by M-H and many other procedures that use simple total test raw or scaled score, and thereby control for Type I error rates. Additionally, SIBTEST explores DIF in a model-free context, making it more independent of a given testing environment than are other approaches. Technically, this feature also constrains SIBTEST as a nonparametric approach, which may actually be an advantage in DIF work.

The SIBTEST DIF procedure addresses the standardization of item identification across tests. The concern here is that a uniform criterion or condition be defined for the item phenomenon. This is shown by its focus on psychometric dimensionality in tests rather than mere identification of aberrant functioning among a set of items. Accordingly, SIBTEST is deliberately grounded in cognitive theory. Essentially, the idea of conducting a SIBTEST is that DIF is evidenced when unidimensionality for a given item is violated. In other words, SIBTEST proffers a procedure to access DIF in items independent of their impact.

To accommodate this interpretation, the matching of groups is presumed to be distributed on a latent, dependent variable, and the DIF presumes multidimensionality as its prima facie evidence. Furthermore, by SIBTEST the tested construct occupies a single dimension in Euclidean space and DIF items evidence at least one additional dimension, which is referred to as the "secondary dimension." The advantage of this approach is both practical and theoretical in that

> SIBTEST analysis allows the user to assert that when bias/DIF is present, then it is the presence or absence of user presumptions about validity made prior to the analysis that then allows the user to decide whether the detected bias/DIF is bias or is DIF. (Shealy & Stout, 1993, p. 159)

This feature of SIBTEST makes it especially appropriate during test development for test developers and psychometricians. Also, such attention during the early stages in developing an assessment program can provide useful information to test users and policymakers as they consider how scores may be meaningfully interpreted.

Another advantage of SIBTEST is its efficiency: Many items can be appraised simultaneously, making it useful in long tests (see Gierl, Gotzmann, & Boughton, 2004). SIBTEST is widely used today; however, some researchers (see Fildago, Ferreres, & Muniz, 2005; Finch, 2005) have pointed out that most research on SIBTEST involves simulated data rather than actual examinee performance. Regardless, the procedure is apparently effective in addressing Type I error rates in DIF work (Klockars & Lee, 2008).

Last, analysis of SIBTEST is commonly accompanied by graphics to illustrate differences between reference and focal groups at different ranges of a test's scale. An illustrative graphic is given in Figure 8.1, along with explanation of a companion procedure—Dorans's Standardization—where the graphic is even more relevant.

Dorans's Standardization

Dorans and Kulick (1983) directly address standards in DIF work as an alternative to the M-H procedure; this is referred to as "the standardization approach," or "Dorans's standardization." This approach is focused on making DIF findings more interpretable, unlike the M-H procedure, which focuses more on statistical power. Dorans and Kulick (1986) demonstrated the utility of this standardization approach by first applying it to the large-scale, national SAT test, where it remained in principal use for many years.

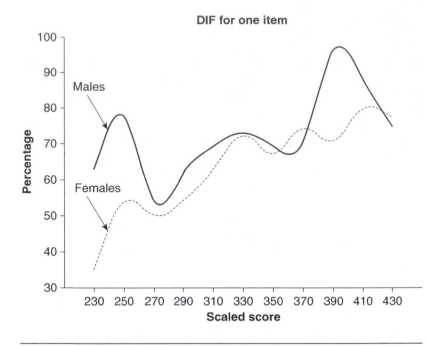

Figure 8.1 Illustration of Standardization Procedures for an Item

As with all DIF procedures, both Dorans's standardization and M-H begin with matching the focal and reference groups on ability. Both DIF techniques allow any credible matching criterion to be used; however, in practice, total test score is nearly always employed for matching. Both approaches configure data for analysis into 2 × 2 contingency tables (one for each score level), exactly as described above for M-H procedures. As with M-H, for Dorans's standardization, the reference group is considered to provide baseline data—that is, the expected performance for the item at each ability level. It is after this step that Dorans's standardization begins to differ from M-H. When extracting information about group performance from the contingency tables, in contrast to the odds-ratio approach of the M-H, Dorans's standardization employs differences in absolute proportion (i.e., percent) correct as the information. DIF is interpreted when the standardized *p*-value difference between the reference and focal groups is detected. And scatterplots of the percent correct regressed onto the total score scale can be prepared for each item, giving a visual preview of DIF.

Graphics play an important role in interpreting the results of the standardization procedure. For example, Figure 8.1 shows DIF from one item, the one that was used to illustrate M-H procedures. In the figure, two groups are contrasted by separately plotting the percentage of examinees in each group who responded correctly to the item at multiple score points. This arrangement of data is more complete than simple multiple-groups comparison; and, in fact, the display reveals a more complex relationship between item response and gender than was available by M-H. From the text above it is clear that M-H groups are fitted to categories by an odds ratio. The M-H approach has the effect of masking differences because each group is assigned to a category without further consideration.

CHAPTER 9. IRT-BASED METHODS

This section describes developments in DIF methods based on IRT (see Hambleton & Swaminathan, 1985; Hambleton, Swaminathan, & Rogers, 1991; Lord & Novick, 1968; Osterlind, 2006). We do not describe all aspects of IRT, as our focus here is on explaining only fundamental concepts of IRT useful in DIF investigation, such as the role of item parameters and how to use ICCs and item response functions (IRFs). Such background explanation is necessary to illustrate how DIF is explored within an IRT framework. This section is divided into three subsections. First, we begin by describing IRT generally, and its role in modern educational and psychological measurement, with an emphasis on how IRT methods are used to detect DIF. Next, we take a closer look at how IRT methods are used to detect DIF in dichotomously (binary) scored test items. Finally, we review a number of relatively recent advances using IRT models to detect DIF in polytomously scored test items.

Obviously, a full treatment of IRT is beyond the scope of this book. There are, however, a number of rich resources available for learning more about IRT. Embretson and Reise (2000), for example, provide an overview of IRT for educators and other social scientists. Hambleton and Swaminathan (1985) and Hambleton et al. (1991) offer two very accessible, book-length introductions to the topic. Also, a classic treatment can be found in *Applications of Item Response Theory to Practical Testing Problems* (Lord, 1980). Yet another informative source is the user's manual accompanying the suite of IRT computer programs offered by Scientific Software International: *IRT From SSI: BILOG-MG, MULTILOG, PARSCALE, TESTFACT* (du Toit, 2003).

Over the past two decades, a number of IRT methods have been developed to detect DIF. IRT methods have proven useful for both conceptualizing and assessing DIF by examining between-group differences in a test item's, or a set of test items', characteristics (e.g., their relative difficulty or their power to discriminate between those who are low or high on the measured construct), independent of examinee ability. Both theoretically and procedurally, IRT-based DIF methods provide an opportunity for a more comprehensive investigation of the phenomenon than can be done using CTT. The measurement literature, particularly with respect to educational testing, is rich with well-documented sources on the use of IRT-based methods for detecting DIF (see Clauser & Mazor, 1998; Millsap & Everson, 1993; Osterlind, 2006; Penfield & Camilli, 2007).

IRT Framework

IRT is an approach to educational and psychological measurement that specifies information about examinees' latent constructs (e.g., abilities, proficiencies, competencies, attitudes) and the characteristics of the test items used to represent them. Briefly, IRT addresses two basic, yet distinct, aspects of measurement: (1) estimating the characteristics of the measurement stimuli and (2) drawing inferences of examinees' latent abilities. IRT models are derived from a family of mathematical procedures that are useful for scaling tests as well as for calculating estimates of examinee ability or proficiency. Though the mathematics underlying IRT can be daunting, they have, nonetheless, proven useful in a variety of measurement and assessment contexts. Again, within the IRT framework, the characteristics of each test item are estimated or calibrated independent of an examinee's ability as measured by the latent construct. This is a clear advantage over CTT methods. The item characteristics are scaled and expressed on the same continuum as is the examinee's ability, an advantage, obviously, for detecting DIF.

In an earlier, comprehensive treatment of statistical methods for detecting biased test items, Camilli and Shepard (1994) noted that IRT is well suited for identifying DIF. In their words,

> Item response theory has several advantages over classical measurement theory for the study of differential item functioning. First, IRT estimates of item parameters (such as difficulty and discrimination) are less confounded with sample characteristics than are those of classical measurement theory. Second, the statistical properties of items can be described in a more precise manner, and consequently, when a test item functions differently in two groups, the differences can be described more precisely. Third the statistical properties of items can be more readily graphed with the IRT approach, which speeds and broadens understanding of items showing DIF. (p. 47)

Figure 9.1 presents this idea graphically.

In the figure, the trace lines for two items—often referred to as ICCs— are shown. The representation considers only one item characteristic, item difficulty, in examining DIF. A hypothetical distribution for two distinct groups, the reference and focal groups, is given along the ability or proficiency (θ) scale. By noting the difference in the group mean values, it is apparent that the probabilities for success differ, providing putative evidence of DIF in both items, but much larger for Item 1 than for Item 2. Mere differences in item difficulty, however, are not axiomatically

40

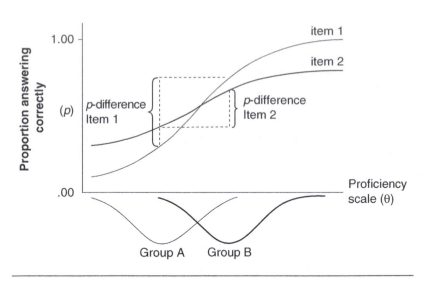

Figure 9.1   Comparison of Two Groups With IRT-Based IRFs

significant. A criterion must be applied to the difference for that determination to hold. Thus, the aim of using IRT in DIF investigations is to determine whether an item assesses the underlying ability or proficiency (θ) similarly for all groups taking the test in the portion of the ability continuum covered by the test item(s).

Within this framework, the probability of a correct response to any given test item is modeled as a function of θ (the underlying or latent ability measured by the test) and one or more item characteristics or item parameters (for a thorough discussion of IRT-based parameter estimation methods, see Baker, 2001). Over the years, a number of variations of IRT models have been developed for use in applied settings. (In this measurement context, a model refers to the mathematical specification of item characteristics and examinee ability estimates and how they relate to the probability of a particular response that may be correct, incorrect, or otherwise graded.) Typically, these IRT models are distinguished by the number of characteristics they estimate about the test items. The three most popular IRT models are the one-, two-, and three-parameter IRT models (abbreviated as 1PL, 2PL, and 3PL, respectively, with "PL" standing for parameter estimates modeled as a logistic function). Below, we describe these three IRT models, discussing the assumptions underlying each. However, before moving on to a description of these models, it is helpful to discuss first the utility of the resulting ICCs or IRFs.

Item Response Curves

In practice, the estimated functions derived by IRT models (for both an item and an examinee) are usually displayed graphically as an item trace line that is placed along the ability and probability continuums. These are labeled as ICCs or sometimes as IRFs because they originate from examinees' observed responses. For purposes of exposition, we will limit our discussion of ICCs to those derived from the 1PL, 2PL, or 3PL models, although many other IRT models exist. The simplest way to explain ICCs is to present a graphical depiction, as was done earlier in Figure 9.1, and here now in Figure 9.2, and describe its parts. Notice immediately the two axes, the abscissa labeled "Trait level" and the ordinate identified as "Probability," $p(\theta)$. The plotted values are shown as a smoothed IRF, technically an ogive. It looks like a cumulative distribution function, and in fact, it is for item characteristics.

In IRT, the proficiency or ability scale (θ) is normalized, placing 0 in the center and symmetrically counting moments away from there. As with any normal frequency, the scale actually can represent the continuum ($-\infty$, $+\infty$), but such a long range is not practical, and usually, four moments (showing the range ±3 SD units) are sufficient to describe the ability range for nearly all populations. The ordinate (vertical axis), in turn, displays the probability of θ from 0 to 1.0, bottom to top. This scale displays the probability estimate from none to absolute along the range (0, 1). Together, the scales allow a trace line

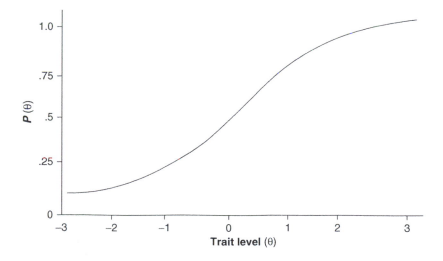

Figure 9.2   Illustrative Item Ogive of Probability as a Function of Trait Level

to describe a functional relationship between the characteristics of an item and the trait level of the examinee. Although it is common for the ogive of ICCs to plot to an S-shaped curve, in some instances, they may assume other forms to convey the information provided by the function. In all cases, however, ogives rise monotonically—that is, their slope is always progressive. In the classic S shape, the curve begins low, rises, and then tapers off as it reaches its upper limit, but the trace line never actually touches either the lower or the upper limit. This tapering off is referred to as an *asymptote*. In functions such as ICCs, there are two asymptotes—a lower and an upper end. The asymptote is where the slope for the ICC trace line is tangential to the lower bound and again to the upper bound (the maximum score of the range, or 1.0). Hence, the trace line approaches, but never reaches, the upper and lower limits—it is said to asymptote. The upper bound is usually not drawn because it is fixed at 1.0 and can be easily imagined.

Now, give attention to the ICCs presented in Figure 9.3. This graphic displays IRFs for three items simultaneously, so that we can see the differences among them. Note that the lower asymptote varies from item to item. For Item 1 it is about .1, while for Item 2 it is slightly above .25, and for Item 3 it is near .5. This lower asymptote has important implications for lower-ability examinees as it indicates the "starting" probability for the item trace line. No measurement is inferred below this starting point.

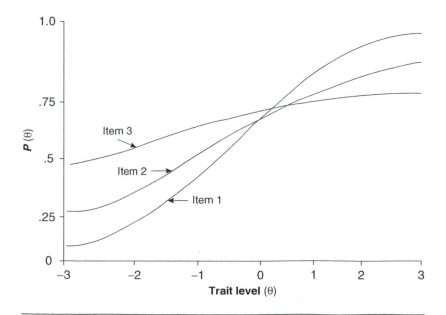

Figure 9.3 Ogives Representing Response Function for Three Items

An interpretation of the different starting points for the various ogives is that Item 1 appears more difficult for low-ability examinees (about 10% probability of responding correctly to the item). In contrast, Item 3 affords nearly 50% probability of an examinee of the same ability obtaining a correct response. For examinees of low ability, these items clearly present varying levels of difficulty. Because examinees at this end of the scale have such a low probability of correct endorsement, this beginning point is referred to as a guessing, or more currently, a pseudochance value. Looking at the other asymptote, one sees that for examinees of high ability (above 2 on the theta scale), there is a parallel interpretation at the upper end of the scale. It is readily apparent which item is easier (i.e., has a high probability of success) for this group.

An aspect of ICCs that is especially important to IRT is the inflection point—that is, half the distance between the upper and lower asymptotes, where the slope is maximal. This represents the point at which the probability of a correct response is .5, when the c parameter (explained later) is equal to 0. In other words, the inflection point is where the odds of an examinee responding correctly to an item change from less than 50% to greater than 50%. (Note, however, that when the c parameter is greater than 0, the inflection point is technically where the probability is $(1 + (c/2))$). Thus, for an easy item, the odds may change at some low point along the theta scale; conversely, for a difficult item, the odds may not change until very high along the ability continuum. When an examinee's ability on the theta scale is also at the item's inflection point, the item is said to be perfectly matched in difficulty to that individual. Figure 9.4 displays the same three ICCs shown earlier in Figure 9.2, but with their inflection points noted on the theta scale. Here, Item 1 has an inflection point at $-.5$. For Items 2 and 3, the inflection points are at 0 and $+1$, respectively.

Studying this threshold point is important to work in IRT and DIF, for a number of reasons. First, it shows the ability level at which the item is maximally discriminating (viz., the slope of the curve is 0). An item that has discriminating odds different from .5 yields less information about ability, since the examinee may find the item either too easy or too difficult for meaningful measurement. Given this information, then, we can determine the suitability of presenting a particular item to a given examinee. By the same reasoning, threshold is also important as an indicator of the item's difficulty level, as denoted along the theta scale. With this as background, we present a brief description of the three most commonly used IRT models.

The One-Parameter Model

The 1PL IRT model is often referred to as the Rasch model after the Danish mathematician Georg Rasch (1960). In the 1PL model, only the test items'

44

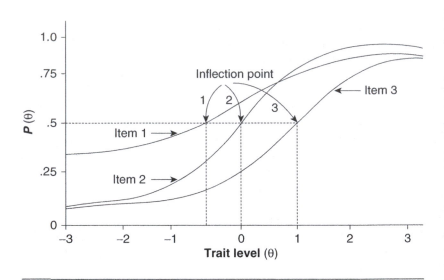

Figure 9.4 Ogives for Three Items Noting Inflection Point Differences Along Trait Scale

difficulty parameters are estimated. (In this model, the items' discrimination parameters are treated as fixed as a constant and, thus, are constrained to be equal across items.) The central psychometric consideration in the 1PL model is directed toward determining the difficulty of the test item presented to an examinee for endorsement. Thus, when an examinee responds to a set of items conceived in this way, his or her underlying trait level is directly manifest. It follows, then, that a correct response to a difficult test item suggests higher trait levels and, conversely, incorrect responses are manifestations of lower trait levels. Although the 1PL model has theoretical appeal, it is often difficult to put into good use because it demands much of the test items and presumes that item responses are a function only of the item's difficulty and not other characteristics. In the 1PL model, the odds of a correct response by an examinee on item i are as given in Equation 9.1:

$$\frac{\theta_a^*}{b_i^*}. \tag{9.1}$$

The asterisk indicates that ability is not independent of item difficulty. Additionally, the odds for an event occurring are defined as $P/(1 - P)$. On a test, the chances for a correct response are expressed as the ratio of the probability of a correct response to the probability of an incorrect response. Thus, the equivalence of the ability odds in terms of the odds of a correct response can be represented by Equation 9.2:

$$\frac{\theta_a^*}{b_i^*} = \frac{P_i(\theta_a)}{1 - P_i(\theta_a)}. \tag{9.2}$$

The expression can be simplified to Equation 9.3:

$$P_i(\theta_a) = \frac{\theta_a^*}{\theta_a^* + b_i^*}. \tag{9.3}$$

Two critical assumptions underpin the 1PL model: First, all items discriminate equally and, second, the pseudochance parameter (guessing) is defined as 0. Then, by setting values for examinee ability and item difficulty, as in Equations 9.4 and 9.5, the 1PL model assumes the form of Equation 9.6:

$$\theta_a^* = e^{D\bar{a}\theta_a}. \tag{9.4}$$

$$b_i^* = e^{D\bar{a}b_i}. \tag{9.5}$$

$$P_i(\theta_a) = \frac{e^{D\bar{a}\theta_a}}{e^{D\bar{a}\theta_a} + e^{D\bar{a}b_i}}. \tag{9.6}$$

Also, the 1PL model implies that examinees with the same number of items correct will have the same θ value, regardless of having answered different items. It is also significant to note that, by reduction, Equation 9.6 is equivalent to the traditional IRT model expressed in Equation 9.3. Thus, with the added assumptions about the 1PL, or Rasch, model, it too can be considered within the family of traditional IRT models.

The Two-Parameter Model

In the 1950s and again later, Birnbaum (1958, 1968) suggested a nonlinear, logistic model to describe two distinct item parameters. The two parameters are (1) item discrimination and (2) item difficulty. To understand these characteristics for items, first look at the parameters graphically, which will aid in understanding the mathematical definition. Figure 9.5 displays an ICC with these two characteristics for each of two items, labeled Item 1 and Item 2.

Figure 9.5 ICCs With Identical Inflection Points but Different Slopes

Notice that the ICCs are not identical. They have different slopes, although both curves inflect at $\theta = 0$, and $P = .5$. Again, as θ increases, the likelihood of a correct response also increases. It is evident in the figure that the slope reflects this feature for items. The differences in slopes for the two items reveal a disparity in discrimination for examinees of varying ability. For Item 1, discrimination is gradual for persons with low ability; then, at about the value of $\theta = -1$, the item's discriminating characteristic rises more steeply, until at about $\theta = +1$, the item's ability to discriminate fades for higher-ability examinees. If we contrast this with Item 2, we see that all along the theta scale the discrimination is much less pronounced, despite the fact that it follows the general form of Item 1's slope. This item characteristic is referred to as the discrimination parameter (or the a parameter). When the slope of an item is especially steep at any one point along the theta scale, the resultant ICC will assume the form of a Guttman scale (Guttman, 1950). Studying the discriminating properties of test items using ICCs is fundamental to the use of IRT in scaling and test development.

Two other items with still different characteristics are shown in Figure 9.6. Here, they are labeled Item 3 and Item 4. Here, we see that the slopes of Items 3 and 4 are virtually identical in the middle but that the inflection points (and hence, the thresholds) are far apart on the theta scale. In other words, the left-to-right shift of the ICCs is what differentiates Items 3 and 4, not their slopes. Clearly, then, for equally able examinees, Item 4 is more difficult since it is located higher along the theta scale, despite the fact that

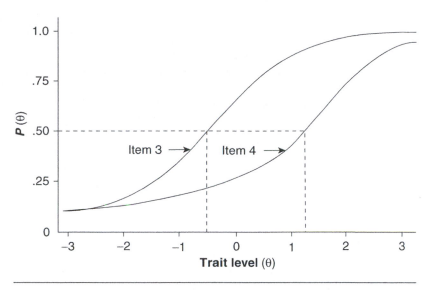

Figure 9.6 Two Items Showing Difference in Difficulty

the items' discrimination parameters are fairly similar. This difference in position along the theta scale for the ICC shows a divergence in difficulty; hence, this parameter is called the difficulty parameter (or the *b* parameter).

Sometimes, in IRT, an item difficulty value is referred to as a location parameter, because it locates the θ value at the point at which the probability function is equal to $.5[P_i(\theta) = .5]$.

The Three-Parameter Model

The 3PL model is used in assessment programs less often than either the 1PL or the 2PL models. Nevertheless, having a clear understanding of this model is important for a more complete picture of the ICCs. The 3PL model includes item-level parameters of the items' discrimination (*a*), difficulty (*b*), and susceptibility to guessing (*c*). This third item characteristic adds to the 2PL model in an attempt to model a response selection strategy used by very low-ability examinees. This parameter, the *c* parameter, is referred to as the pseudochance level but is often simply called the "guessing parameter." The full 3PL model is shown in Equation 9.7. All terms of the equation are as defined for Equation 9.6, with of course the addition of the *c* parameter. The function represented in Equation 9.7 describes an S-shaped curve that specifies the probability of a correct response as a function of θ. Thus, the exact form of the S-shaped curve for any particular item, naturally, will depend on the values of the a, b, and c parameters. And as before, the resulting curve is commonly referred to as an ICC or an IRF. The constant D is fixed at 1.7 and serves the purpose of scaling the 3PL model to be very close in form to the normal ogive model (Osterlind, 2006).

In the ICC for a 3PL IRT model, the c parameter is the lower asymptote, the bound of the curve as it approaches 0. Technically, c is the value the probability takes at the lowest numerical value of θ. Graphically, it is the point at which the ogive begins, and it appears on the left side of the ICC (compare Figure 9.1, 9.2, or 9.3). The 3PL logistic model is, perhaps, the most general and widely used IRT model, especially for dichotomously scored test items. The 3PL model is represented in Equation 9.7.

$$P_i(\theta) = c_i + (1 - c_i) \frac{e^{Da_i(\theta - b_i)}}{1 + e^{Da_i(\theta - b_i)}} \qquad (i = 1, 2, \ldots, n). \qquad (9.7)$$

In the 3PL model, the a parameter represents the item discrimination index, the b parameter refers to the difficulty of the test item, and c corresponds to the pseudoguessing parameter of the test item—that is, the probability of a correct response for an examinee with asymptotically low ability or proficiency.

A graphical representation of the full 3PL, with all the most common item characteristics identified, is given in Figure 9.7.

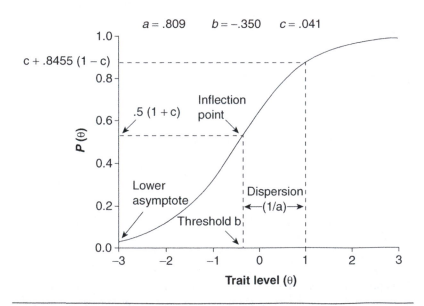

Figure 9.7 Aspects of 3PL Scaling for a Single Item

DIF Methods Based on IRT

DIF detection methods based on IRT provide a useful and comprehensive approach to investigating differences in item parameters across groups. As Clauser and Mazor (1998) and others (Camilli & Shephard, 1994; Penfield & Camilli, 2007; Zumbo,1999) have noted, IRT scaling properties provide us with a natural, straightforward means of studying DIF in a particular test item. Although a number of IRT-based approaches are available for identifying between-group differences in item parameters, no single method is the best. It is also important to note that the IRT framework provides us with two interpretations of DIF: (1) between-group differences in the ICCs and (2) between-group differences in an item's parameters. Penfield and Camilli (2007) remind us that both interpretations of DIF have been used to develop methods for detecting DIF. In general, essentially all the various statistical methods share essentially the same conceptual null hypothesis: That is, the item parameters are invariant across the reference and focal groups (Clauser & Mazor, 1998).

Differences in Item Parameters

A more straightforward approach to testing for DIF is contrasting the item parameters, particularly the b parameter, for the reference and focal groups. Following Lord (1980), the simplest statistic for testing the null hypothesis that the b parameters are equal for the reference and focal groups is given by

$$d = \frac{(\hat{b}_R - \hat{b}_F)}{SE(\hat{b}_R - \hat{b}_F)}, \tag{9.8}$$

where $SE\,(\hat{b}_R - \hat{b}_F)$ represents the standard error of the difference between the b estimates for the reference and the focal groups, given by

$$SE(\hat{b}_R - \hat{b}_F) = \sqrt{[SE(\hat{b}_R)]^2 + [SE(\hat{b}_F)]^2}. \tag{9.9}$$

This test statistic, d, is distributed approximately as standard normal and, therefore, provides a test of the null hypothesis H_0: $b_R = b_F$.

Indeed, if the 1PL model fits the data, as is often the case in many operational testing programs, then the test statistic d offers a useful and straightforward test of the null hypothesis of no DIF. On the other hand, if either the 2PL or the 3PL model is more appropriate, then only testing the differences between b_R and b_F may be somewhat misleading. In this case, it was suggested by Lord (1980) that a chi-square test of the simultaneous differences between the b and a parameters may be a more appropriate test for DIF. Thus, if the differences in the estimated parameters are represented as

$$\hat{v}' = (\hat{a}_R - \hat{a}_F, \ \hat{b}_R - \hat{b}_F),$$ (9.10)

then the following statistic can be computed:

$$\chi_L^2 = \hat{v}' S^{-1} \hat{v}.$$ (9.11)

In Equation 9.11, S represents the estimated variance-covariance matrix of the between-group difference in the a- and b-parameter estimates. Thus, assuming the null hypothesis of no DIF, the obtained value of x_L^2 is distributed as a chi-square variable with 2 degrees of freedom. Interested readers should consult Lord (1980) and Camilli and Shepard (1994) for more detailed discussions of this approach to investigating DIF by testing for invariant item parameters.

Likelihood Ratio Test

A likelihood ratio test has been developed recently for use in IRT-based DIF studies. This approach compares the likelihood when a particular test item's parameters are constrained to be invariant for the reference and focal groups with the likelihood when the parameters of the same studied item are allowed to vary between the reference and focal groups. Following the description offered recently by Penfield and Camilli (2007), one indicates the likelihood obtained when the item under investigation has parameters constrained to be invariant across the reference and focal groups by $L(C)$ and the likelihood obtained when the item's parameters are free to vary across groups by $L(A)$; thus, a likelihood ratio test is available by computing

$$G^2 = 2\ln\left[\frac{L(A)}{L(C)}\right].$$ (9.12)

As described elsewhere (see Thissen, Steinberg, & Wainer, 1993), the statistic G^2 is distributed approximately as a chi-square variable. The interested reader should consult these sources for more details.

From a practical and procedural perspective, then, those interested in DIF, as we said earlier, typically look to determine whether a studied item's b parameter is estimated similarly for the reference and focal groups. When using widely available programs for estimating IRT parameters, such as BILOG-MG, the a parameter is estimated but constrained to be equal across groups. Again, this is necessary to locate the item on the theta scale.

Accordingly, when investigating DIF, using BILOG-MG, a 1PL model is instantiated. For purposes of exposition, a sample syntax file for DIF calculation by BILOG-MG on the College BASE examination is given in Figure 9.8. Additional information and commands for the syntax and the FORTRAN command line are provided in the BILOG-MG user's manual (du Toit, 2003).

In general, these item parameters are represented by separate ICCs, one each for the focal and reference groups. Figures 9.9 through 9.14 display DIF-related statistics for the same item(s) from College BASE. Figure 9.9 displays the ICCs and associated item information curves for a reference and a focal group (females in the bottom panel and males in the top panel, respectively) for one item.

It is important to note that the b values (given at the top of each ICC and located by the arrow on the ability scale) are far apart between the groups. Significant differences in ICCs can be interpreted as evidence that DIF evidence exists (Lord, 1980). For interested readers, the mathematics of calculating these values are described by Thissen et al. (1993), who also demonstrate its execution in several other computer programs, including MULTILOG, LISCOMP, SPSS LOGLINEAR, LOGIMO, and BIMAIN.

Other IRT-based methods also compute statistics between the groups, first separately for each group and then together. For marginal maximum likelihood estimation, BILOG-MG can be employed. Such calibrated values are displayed in Figures 9.10 and 9.11. In Figure 9.10, traditional item indices are calculated, first for each group and then for the total sample. These are followed by the IRT-based item parameter estimates (compare Figure 19.11).

```
College BASE data- Form LP
>COMMENT
Sample run with CB data, form LP for DIF. Two groups are used: Male & Female
The needed files (beyond this *.blm file are labeled:
        the data file              CB2data.dat
        the answer key             CB2KEY.Key
        the omit file (coded as 9)  CB2omit.omt
Scoring phase is not invoked as it is invalid for DIF analysis; but PLOT command is used.
After the data is run, use Run-->Plot to activate the graphics module.

>GLOBAL DFName = 'C:\Program Files\bilogmg\Examples\CB2data.dat',
        NPArm = 1;
>LENGTH NITems = (41);
>INPUT NTOtal = 41, NALt = 5,NIDchar = 8, NGRoup = 2,
        KFName = 'C:\Program Files\bilogmg\Examples\CB2key.KEY',
        OFName = 'C:\Program Files\bilogmg\Examples\CB2omit.OMT',
        DIF;
>ITEMS INAmes = (ITEM001(1)ITEM041);
>TEST1 TNAme = 'CB_LP', INUmber = (1(1)41);
>GROUP1 GNAme = 'MALES', LENgth = 41,INUmbers = (1(1)41);
>GROUP2 GNAme = 'FEMALES', LENgth = 41, INUmbers = (1(1)41);
(8A1, 3X, I1, 33X, 42A1)
>CALIE PLot = 1.0000;
```

Figure 9.8   Illustrative BILOG-MG Syntax for DIF

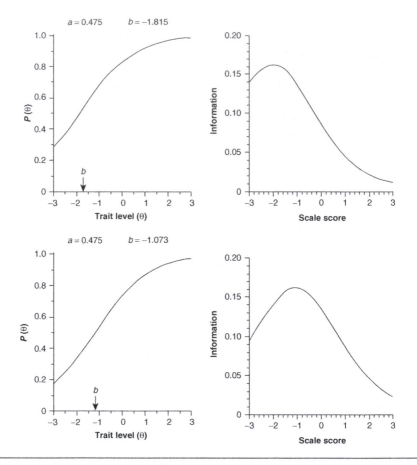

Figure 9.9 ICCs for One Item for Two Groups: Reference (*Top Panels*) and Focal (*Bottom Panels*)

To make meaningful comparisons, the IRT-based threshold values in the reference group are linearly transformed, by an adjustment, to the scale for the focal group. This is important because it puts the parameter estimates for both groups on the same (and, consequently, comparable) scale. This adjustment factor is displayed in Figure 9.12.

Then, the adjusted threshold values for the focal and reference groups are calculated, as displayed in Figure 9.13. And, finally, the differences between values for the focal and reference groups are given, as shown in Figure 9.14. The difference values are viewed as a relative amount, with large differences indicating DIF.

```
ITEM STATISTICS FOR GROUP:    1    MALES
                                          ITEM*TEST CORRELATION
ITEM   NAME     #TRIED  #RIGHT    PCT   LOGIT/1.7  PEARSON BISERIAL
------------------------------------------------------------------
  1    ITEM01   953.0   748.0    0.785   -0.76      0.181   0.254
  2    ITEM02   953.0   792.0    0.831   -0.94      0.187   0.278
  3    ITEM03   953.0   818.0    0.858   -1.06      0.152   0.236

ITEM STATISTICS FOR GROUP:    2    FEMALES

                                          ITEM*TEST CORRELATION
ITEM   NAME     #TRIED  #RIGHT    PCT   LOGIT/1.7  PEARSON BISERIAL
------------------------------------------------------------------
  1    ITEM01  3933.0  2690.0    0.684   -0.45      0.236   0.309
  2    ITEM02  3933.0  3272.0    0.832   -0.94      0.204   0.304
  3    ITEM03  3933.0  3511.0    0.893   -1.25      0.190   0.319

ITEM STATISTICS FOR MULTIPLE GROUPS   CB_LP
                                          ITEM*TEST CORRELATION
ITEM   NAME     #TRIED  #RIGHT    PCT   LOGIT/1.7  PEARSON BISERIAL
------------------------------------------------------------------
  1    ITEM01  4886.0  3438.0    0.704   -0.51      0.228   0.301
  2    ITEM02  4886.0  4064.0    0.832   -0.94      0.200   0.298
  3    ITEM03  4886.0  4329.0    0.886   -1.21      0.180   0.296
```

Figure 9.10   Classical Item Statistics for Reference and Focal Groups

```
GROUP 1 MALES ; ITEM PARAMETERS AFTER CYCLE 3
ITEM   INTERCEPT   SLOPE    THRESHOLD LOADING ASYMPTOTE  CHISQ   DF
         S.E.       S.E.       S.E.    S.E.     S.E.     (PROB)
------------------------------------------------------------------
ITEM01 | 0.862  | 0.475  | -1.815  | 0.429  | 0.000  |   5.4   9.0
       | 0.048* | 0.004* |  0.101* | 0.004* | 0.000* | (0.7983)
       |        |        |         |        |        |
ITEM02 | 1.054  | 0.475  | -2.220  | 0.429  | 0.000  |   2.5   9.0
       | 0.052* | 0.004* |  0.110* | 0.004* | 0.000* | (0.9810)
       |        |        |         |        |        |
ITEM03 | 1.186  | 0.475  | -2.498  | 0.429  | 0.000  |   4.4   9.0
       | 0.056* | 0.004* |  0.118* | 0.004* | 0.000* | (0.8803)

GROUP 2 FEMALES; ITEM PARAMETERS AFTER CYCLE 3
ITEM   INTERCEPT   SLOPE    THRESHOLD LOADING ASYMPTOTE  CHISQ   DF
         S.E.       S.E.       S.E.    S.E.     S.E.     (PROB)
------------------------------------------------------------------
ITEM01 | 0.509  | 0.475  | -1.073  | 0.429  | 0.000  |   4.7   9.0
       | 0.021* | 0.004* |  0.045* | 0.004* | 0.000* | (0.8578)
       |        |        |         |        |        |
ITEM02 | 1.040  | 0.475  | -2.191  | 0.429  | 0.000  |   1.0   9.0
       | 0.026* | 0.004* |  0.055* | 0.004* | 0.000* | (0.9994)
       |        |        |         |        |        |
ITEM03 | 1.364  | 0.475  | -2.873  | 0.429  | 0.000  |   6.7   9.0
       | 0.031* | 0.004* |  0.066* | 0.004* | 0.000* | (0.6719)
```

Figure 9.11   IRT-Based Item Statistics for Reference and Focal Groups

```
PARAMETER          MEAN   STN DEV
- - - - - - - - - - - - - - - - - - - - - - - - - - - -
GROUP:    1  NUMBER OF ITEMS:     41
THRESHOLD      -1.002    0.928
GROUP:    2  NUMBER OF ITEMS:     41
THRESHOLD      -0.877    0.944
- - - - - - - - - - - - - - - - - - - - - - - - - - - -



THRESHOLD MEANS

GROUP           ADJUSTMENT
- - - - - - - - - - - - - - - - - - - - -
  1              0.000
  2              0.125
- - - - - - - - - - - - - - - - - - - - -
```

Figure 9.12   Adjustment of IRT Parameter Estimate

One way to test these values is with a traditional Student's t test. Here, the numerator is the difference between the groups on the b parameters for a given item, and the denominator is the square root of the sum of the two standard errors, which is demonstrated in Equation 9.13 (S. E. Embretson, personal communication, April 2003):

$$t_{DIF} = \frac{b_F - b_R}{\sqrt{SE_F + SE_R}}, \tag{9.13}$$

where b_F is the difficulty parameter for the focal group and b_R is the adjusted difficulty parameter for the reference group.

Yet another way to estimate the significance of DIF is to subtract the focal group's adjusted b from the reference group's, and if its absolute value is more than 2 or 3 standard errors (which are given for each item in the BILOG-MG output), then the difference is presumed to be significant. As we noted earlier, the criterion of a difference between groups of 2 standard errors may result in overidentifying items as DIF; hence, some researchers use the more conservative criterion of a difference greater than 3 standard errors. In either case, the standard error approach is reasonable as the metric for difference scores by BILOG-MG is a z score, a standardized unit.

MODEL FOR GROUP DIFFERENTIAL ITEM FUNCTIONING:
ADJUSTED THRESHOLD VALUES

ITEM	GROUP 1	GROUP 2		ITEM	GROUP 1	GROUP 2
ITEM01	-1.815	-1.198		ITEM22	-2.112	-2.005
	0.101*	0.045*			0.113*	0.052*
ITEM02	-2.220	-2.315		ITEM23	-0.376	-0.312
	0.110*	0.055*			0.088*	0.043*
ITEM03	-2.498	-2.998		ITEM24	-0.695	-0.731
	0.118*	0.066*			0.088*	0.043*

Figure 9.13   Adjusted Threshold Values

MODEL FOR GROUP DIFFERENTIAL ITEM FUNCTIONING:
GROUP THRESHOLD DIFFERENCES

ITEM	GROUP 2-1		ITEM	GROUP 2-1	ITEM	GROUP 2-1
ITEM01	0.618		ITEM15	-0.405	ITEM29	0.079
	0.110*			0.095*		0.101*
ITEM02	-0.096		ITEM16	0.007	ITEM30	-0.059
	0.123*			0.096*		0.113*
ITEM03	-0.500		ITEM17	-0.182	ITEM31	0.354
	0.135*			0.095*		0.123*

Figure 9.14   Group Differences After Threshold Values Are Adjusted

Area Measures

Estimates of effect size and/or of statistical significance are based on comparing item parameters; for example, differences between both the difficulty and the discrimination parameters can be quantified by estimating the difference in area between the ICCs for the two groups (Raju, 1988; Rudner and Gagne & Gagne, 2001). An important concern, however, is how to determine whether a difference is significant. Sometimes, it can be determined by merely "eyeballing" the differences and making a reasonable judgment, but a more precise method is desired that uses some test statistics. One popular method, the signed area (SA) effect size index, was first introduced by Rudner and Gagne (2001) and developed further by Raju (1988) and Raju, van der Linden, and Fleer (1995), who demonstrated how to estimate the area between two ICCs. This SA effect size index is represented by the following integral

$$SA = \int_{-\infty}^{\infty} [P(Y=1|\theta, G=R) - P(Y=1|\theta, G=F)]d\theta. \quad (9.14)$$

Assuming that the c parameter is invariant across groups, SA can be expressed as a function of the item parameters for the reference and focal groups such that

$$SA = (1-c)(b_F - b_R). \quad (9.15)$$

Under the assumption of invariant c parameters, SA is independent of the a parameter, even in those cases where the a parameter is not invariant across groups (Penfield & Camilli, 2007; Raju, 1988). DIF, as indexed by SA, is a function of the between-group difference in the item difficulty parameter (b). In addition, larger between-group differences in the b parameter lead to conditional between-group differences in the probability of correct response and, in turn, larger DIF effects. Thus, for the 1PL model, SA is equal to the b-parameter difference between the two groups (i.e., $b_F - b_R$).

Still, researchers should use this with care. As Penfield and Camilli (2007) caution, SA may be misleading in those instances when the a parameter is not invariant across groups and, in particular, if the ICCs cross anywhere on the interval of $-3 \leq \theta \leq 3$. In these instances, the difference between the ICCs will be positive on one side of the point of intersection of the ICCs for the reference and focal groups and negative on the other side, suggesting that the area indices will cancel out. This could lead to attenuated SA values even though there are meaningful differences in the ICCs for the two groups of examinees.

To address this issue, Raju (1988) and his colleagues have proposed considering the unsigned area (UA) between the ICCs of the reference and focal groups, given by the integral

$$UA = \int_{-\infty}^{\infty} [P(Y=1|\theta, G=R) - P(Y=1|\theta, G=F)]d\theta. \quad (9.16)$$

Again, when the c parameter is invariant across groups, the value of UA is equal to

$$UA = (1-C)\left| \frac{2(a_F - a_R)}{Da_Fa_R} \ln\left[1 + \exp\left(\frac{Da_Fa_R(b_F - b_R)}{a_F - a_R} \right) \right] - (b_F - b_R) \right|. \quad (9.17)$$

The form of UA shown in Equation 9.16 can be reduced further when the a parameter is also invariant across the two groups, and is equal to

$$UA = (1 - C)|b_F - b_R|. \qquad (9.18)$$

While the SA and UA indices make use of the IRT framework to provide theoretical measures of DIF effect size, they do not offer an efficient method for testing the null hypothesis of no DIF. One limitation of these area measures is that they often fail to take into account the distribution of examinees across the theta scale, thus producing misleading interpretations of the size of the observed DIF for specific groups or classes of examinees. In addition, SA and UA measures require estimation of the respective item-level parameters for each group separately, which taxes the data because sample sizes are often insufficient for estimating stable item parameters, particularly for the focal group. Nevertheless, we present them here because investigators ought to be aware of their utility for interpreting the more commonly used DIF statistics. According to Penfield and Camilli (2007), SA and UA area measures

> describe important theoretical relationships between the magnitude of DIF and between-group differences in the item parameters, relationships that are often used in interpreting the results of DIF analyses and simulating responses containing varying levels of DIF in conducting research related to DIF detection statistics. (p. 131)

IRT Approaches for Detecting DIF in Polytomous Items

As with binary scored (dichotomous) test items, the literature contains a number of methods for identifying DIF in polytomous items (see, e.g., Penfield & Lam, 2000; Potenza & Dorans, 1995). Many are extensions of the methods used with dichotomous items, even though conceptually DIF in polytomous items is not as straightforward because of multiple score points or scoring categories. With polytomously scored test items, for example, the conditional dependence between the item response and the grouping variable G may be a function of the between-group difference in the conditional probability of any one of the response categories. As with binary test items, the IRT framework, however, is useful for estimating the probability of each response option as a function of θ, examinee proficiency or ability. Many of the proposed polytomous IRT models are variations of either the generalized partial credit model (GPCM) or the graded response model (GRM). The GPCM (Muraki, 1992) is widely used in practice. The GPCM estimates the probability of attaining response option j, given the attainment of response option $j-1$ (represented by n_j), using the 2PL model

$$n_j(\theta) = \frac{\exp[Da(\theta - b_j)}{1 - \exp[Da(\theta - b_j)}.$$ (9.19)

Briefly, and relying on notation first presented by Penfield and Camilli (2007), for a particular test item with a number (r) of response categories, we denote a particular response category by j, where $j = 0, 1, \ldots, J$, such that $J = r - 1$. There will be J such adjacent category probability functions, one each for $j = 1, 2, \ldots, J$. Thus, the difficulty of shifting from category $j - 1$ to category j is estimated by the b_j parameter—with higher values associated with the θ estimates.

Similarly, Samejima's (1997) GRM denotes the conditional cumulative probability of response option $Y \geq j > 0$ in the following:

$$y_j(\theta) = \frac{\exp[Da(\theta - b_j)}{1 - \exp[Da(\theta - b_j)}.$$ (9.20)

And like Muraki's (1992) GPCM, Samejima's (1997) GRM assumes J such cumulative probability functions, and as the parameters for b_j increase, a higher θ value is needed for a conditional probability of attaining a least-category j. As we discussed earlier when describing dichotomously scored test items, likelihood ratio tests are also used to detect DIF in polytomously scored test items and can be implemented using MULTILOG 7 (Thissen, Chen, & Bock, 2003). However, Bolt (2005), in a study using Monte Carlo methods, reported that the likelihood ratio test for the GRM may be limited by inflated Type I errors, particularly when the data are not a good fit with the GRM.

CHAPTER 10. LOGISTIC REGRESSION

Logistic regression in DIF work invokes a probability function that is estimated by methods of maximum likelihood (see Hosmer & Lemeshow, 1989). In this DIF procedure, the dependent variable is categorical and represents the likelihood of responding to an item in an estimably predictable manner, specifically as correct or incorrect (for binary items) or on an ordinal scale (for polytomous items). The response is conditioned on group membership, which is dummy coded for the reference and focal groups. Other independent variables are the matching criterion and an interaction term. The probability of P and Q (i.e., $1 - P$) corresponds to the proportion of examinees responding correctly and incorrectly to the item, respectively, in a manner parallel to what we saw earlier with M-H procedures. This representation means, too, that the variance of the dependent variable is equal to $P(1 - P)$ or PQ. Also, since the population means of the Ys at each level and the Xs are not on a straight line, the relationship is nonlinear. Furthermore, as the errors are not normally distributed, the assumption of homoscedasticity is untenable. As a consequence, ordinary least squares will not appropriately estimate the population parameters; and hence, the scale for analysis is transformed by logs, and the solution is achieved by maximum likelihood.

These are the hallmark features of logistic regression, and they work to advantage in DIF analyses. One such advantage is that expressing the groups' responses to an outcome for an item (either correct or incorrect) as a probability is consistent with psychological and educational test score interpretations. Remember, despite our many sophisticated statistics, mental appraisal is not an exact science, so *probability* is an appropriate term. There are also practical advantages in using likelihood functions in DIF work. For one, here the normality assumptions for the data are relaxed, making logistic regression versatile for researchers exploring DIF in a wide variety of real-world contexts where smaller sample sizes are common and sample distributions are often skewed.

Another advantage of logistic regression in DIF work is that researchers can explore for either uniform or nonuniform DIF. In fact, usually both are considered simultaneously. Furthermore, the method is not limited to dichotomously scored items. Polytomous items may be investigated, although usually with just a three-group solution (see French & Miller, 1996). Still, even this flexibility makes the procedure available to many Likert and Likert-type items as well as for essay scores.

Keep in mind, however, that the concern in logistic regression is with the scoring model (e.g., binary, multicategory) and not the format for items, per se. In other words, for binary regression solutions, it does not matter whether the items are formatted as multiple choice, as true versus false, or in some other dichotomously scored format. For polytomous items, the categorical dependent variable supports either a two-group or a three-group solution as a practical limit despite the fact that regression theory allows solutions with more than three categories. Hence, when Likert and Likert-type items (or other multicategory formats) are explored for DIF by logistic regression, the researcher may need to collapse some response categories so that only two or three categories remain for the analyses.

Last, consistent with the psychological interpretations discussed above, DIF by logistic regression adheres to the common psychometric presumption that the response to an item reflects an examinee's placement along a continuum of latent ability. The examinee's latent ability continuum is extant even when the item used to appraise it is scored dichotomously. The M-H procedures, as well as IRT and other IRT-based methods, such as full-information factor analysis, rely on this presupposition.

The Logistic Regression DIF Expression

Now, we explain some common approaches for conducting DIF analyses with logistic regression. The regression expression takes the form

$$Y = \beta_0 + \beta_1 X_1 + \beta_2 X_2 + \beta_3 X_1 X_2. \tag{10.1}$$

The Y term on the left-hand side of Equation 10.1 is, of course, the outcome and the dependent variable. On the right-hand side of Equation 10.1, the numbered βs are the respective coefficient weights for each independent variable. The intercept is β_0. The intercept represents the probability of a response category (i.e., likelihood in the maximum likelihood solution) when X_1 and X_2 are constrained to 0. The first independent variable, X_1, is the criterion used for matching groups on ability, usually total test score. The variable X_2 is group membership, dummy coded. Interaction between these variables is indicated by $X_1 X_2$.

Differences in probability on the first independent variable connote uniform DIF. Nonuniform DIF is indicated by a nonzero interaction term. The reasoning here is the same as using ability levels as discrete, unordered categories in a factorial analysis of variance.

When Equation 10.1 is expressed with the dependent variable as the natural log of the odds ratio, it is expressed as in Equation 10.2:

$$P(u = 1|\theta) = \frac{e^{(\beta_0 + \beta_1 \theta)}}{[1 + e^{(\beta_0 + \beta_1 \theta)}]}. \tag{10.2}$$

The left-hand side of Equation 10.2 presents the probability of a correct response to the item, conditioned on ability (θ). And DIF can be specified in separate equations for the reference and focal groups, as in Equation 10.3.

$$P(u_{ij} = 1|\theta) = \frac{e^{(\beta_{0j} + \beta_{1j} + \theta_{ij})}}{\left[1 + e^{(\beta_{0j} + \beta_{1j} + \theta_{ij})}\right]}. \tag{10.3}$$

Here, the probability of an individual (i) within a particular group (j) depends on ability. There are two groups: reference and focal. DIF is indicated when examinees of matched ability exhibit a different probability of success on the item. That is to say, when the logistic regression curves are the same, no DIF is inferred. In Equation 10.3, this means that $\beta_{01} = \beta_{02}$ and $\beta_{11} = \beta_{12}$ in each case. When this is not the case (i.e., $\beta_{01} \neq \beta_{02}$ and $\beta_{11} \neq \beta_{12}$), then uniform DIF is inferred. Nonuniform DIF can be inferred when the interaction of ability by group is distinctly indicated or is represented using the formula $\beta_{01} = \beta_{02}$ and $\beta_{11} \neq \beta_{12}$.

For analysis, the variables are entered into the regression equation hierarchically, beginning with the matching criterion (i.e., total score), followed by the group identification variable, and finally the interaction term. The solution is found in the resultant chi-square statistics evaluated with 2 degrees of freedom (i.e., $df = 2$) against the full chi-square distribution. Two degrees of freedom is a calculation from the difference between the $df = 3$ of the interaction and the $df = 1$ from the initial conditioning variable; hence, $df = 2$. The test of independence is establishing whether or not the paired observations of item responses differ from a theoretical distribution.

The same chi-square test with $df = 2$ is used for binary score analysis and ordinal scores. This is appropriate due to the fact that the comparisons between the grouping variable to the conditioning variable (to test uniform DIF) and the interaction variable to the conditioning variable (to test nonuniform DIF) are parallel. It also allows for simultaneous evaluation of both uniform and nonuniform DIF, as noted earlier.

Example of DIF by Logistic Regression

DIF by logistic regression is demonstrated with two multiple-choice items from a test of general achievement. The items—labeled as #4 and #12—are scored dichotomously as 1 for correct and 0 for incorrect. The sample for analysis is 300 examinees in each of two groups: reference and focal. The statistics were performed with SPSS v.16 (SPSS, 2008), and the syntax for analysis was prepared by Zumbo (1999).

Selected output of the analysis for one item is given in Figures 10.1 to 10.3. As before, this is the same item from College BASE, so that the procedures are uniformly illustrated. For descriptive statistics, a cross-tabulation was computed, as displayed in Figure 10.1. Note the chi-square

Item_4*group Crosstabulation

Count

		group		
		Reference	Focal	Total
Item_4	0	300	228	528
	1	53	19	72
	Total	353	247	600

Block 1: Method = Enter

Omnibus Tests of Model Coefficients

		Chi-square	df	Sig.
Step1	Step	133.387	1	.000
	Block	133.387	1	.000
	Model	133.387	1	.000

Model Summary

Step	−2 Log likelihood	Cox & Snell R Square	Nagelkerke R Square
1	306.923[a]	.199	.383

a. Estimation terminated at iteration number 7 because parameter estimates changed by less than .001.

Classification Table[a]

			Predicted		
			Item_4		
Observed			0	1	Percentage Correct
Step1	Item_4	0	514	14	97.3
		1	50	22	30.6
	Overall Percentage				89.3

a. The cut value is .500

Variables in the Equation

		B	S.E.	Wald	df	Sig.	Exp(B)
Step1	Total_score	.247	.027	81.203	1	.000	1.281
	Constant	−21.629	2.255	91.976	1	.000	.000

Figure 10.1 Beginning Block in Logistic Regression Method

value and the Nagelkerke R^2 value in Block 1. This test is for uniform DIF, as is shown by only the grouping variable in the equation.

In Block 2, however, the interaction is included, illustrating a nonuniform DIF, as illustrated in Figure 10.2.

Block 2: Method = Enter
Omnibus Tests of Model Coefficients

		Chi-square	df	Sig.
Step1	Step	.097	2	.952
	Block	.097	2	.952
	Model	133.484	3	.000

Model Summary

Step	−2 Log likelihood	Cox & Snell R Square	Nagelkerke R Square
1	306.826[a]	.199	.384

a. Estimation terminated at iteration number 7 because parameter estimates changed by less than .001.

Classification Table[a]

			Predicted		
			Item_4		
	Observed		0	1	Percentage Correct
Step1	Item_4	0	514	14	97.3
		1	50	22	30.6
	Overall Percentage				89.3

a. The cut value is .500

Variables in the Equation

		B	S.E.	Wald	df	Sig.	Exp(B)
Step1	Total_Score	.248	.049	25.699	1	.000	1.281
	group(1)	−.259	4.848	.003	1	.957	.772
	group(1) by Total_Score	.002	.060	.001	1	.975	1.002
	Constant	−21.594	3.929	30.210	1	.000	.000

Figure 10.2 Ending Block in Logistic Regression Method

The syntax for SPSS is given in Figure 10.3. This syntax can be run for many data sets with only minor modifications. A more complete syntax with provided data sets is offered by Zumbo (1999) on a Web site that accompanies his extensive treatment of the topic: *A Handbook on the Theory and Methods of Differential Item Functioning: Logistic Regression Modeling as a Unitary Framework for Binary and Likert-Type Item Scores.*

COMMENT Computes Crosstabs for descriptive, and chi-squared test (evaluate with
2df) for simultaneous evaluation of uniform and non-uniform DIF.
CROSSTABS
 /TABLES=Item_4 BY group
 /FORMAT=AVALUE TABLES
 /CELLS=COUNT
 /COUNT ROUND CELL.
LOGISTIC REGRESSION VAR=Item_4
 /METHOD=ENTER Total_Score /METHOD=ENTER Group Group*Total_Score
 /CONTRAST (Group)=Indicator
 /CRITERIA PIN(.05) POUT(.10) ITERATE(20) CUT(.5).
EXECUTE.

Figure 10.3   SPSS v. 17 Syntax for Computing Logistic Regression DIF

CHAPTER 11. SPECIALIZED DIF PROCEDU

While the DIF methods described earlier are the ones used most commonly, they are not the only ones available for aberrant item investigation. Indeed, there are circumstances and tests in which a specialized approach may be appropriate, such as when items are polytomously scored or when the concern rests with translated tests. Some of these methods are discussed here.

Polytomously Scored Items

Increasingly, attention is being focused on exploring DIF in polytomously scored items (Koretz & Hamilton, 2006). And researchers are looking at DIF from both unidimensional and multidimensional perspectives. Clearly, the need for such exploration in next-generation tests is necessary, as we note from the ever-larger discrepancies between ethnic groups' performance (Lane & Stone, 2006). Here, we briefly describe two promising new directions for studying DIF and differential test functioning (DTF). The first is an IRT-based approach known as differential functioning of items and tests (DFIT), proposed by Raju and his colleagues in numerous, important studies (Flowers, Oshima, & Raju, 1999; Raju, Oshima, & Wolach, 2005; Raju, van der Linden, & Fleer, 1995). The other is a relatively novel approach that incorporates statistical equivalence testing (Tryon, 2001; Wells, Wollack, & Serlin, 2008) to the challenges of detecting DIF in educational test items.

Additionally, attention to aberrant item functioning in polytomous items is a special concern in performance tests, such as is commonly used in licensing and certification assessment. Commonly, M-H approaches are used here, but special attention must be paid to validity in interpretation of DIF results (Zwick, Donoghue, & Grima, 1993). And the logistic regression framework described earlier has been extended to investigate DIF in polytomous items. One approach, for example, is to recode the polytomous response categories (r) into $J = r - 1$ coded variables. This approach was proposed initially by French and Miller (1996) and has been described in detail by Penfield and Camilli (2007).

Examining DIF in polytomous items begs a question parallel to one in an initial, omnibus finding in factorial ANOVA: Where is the difference located? With polytomous DIF items, this means identifying the score level that contains DIF. DIF may be recognized in just one or more than one level. For example, suppose an item is graded on a four-point continuum, leaving three score levels. The DIF can be evidenced at any or all levels, or it may even be reversed at different score levels. Knowing whether DIF is extant in one or more of the levels is obviously useful information not only for test developers but also for evaluation and other research. One can see this point easily by considering items and assessment exercises that are scored along degrees of proficiency, such as in most writing appraisals.

Particularly with polytomously scored items, pinpointing the score level for DIF can provide further information not only about group differences but also for curriculum evaluation. Furthermore, DIF-related knowing-level information can even provide important clues to learning causes for the DIF. Penfield and Gattamorta (2009) refer to this examination of between-group properties as "differential step functioning" (DSF).

DSF procedures can be employed for all conventional scaling methods used with polytomous items or appraisal exercises, regardless of whether they are based on CTT or IRT. In IRT models, the probability of an examinee obtaining a particular step is calculated for $J = r - 1$ step functions, where r is the number of response options and J the number of step functions. When $r = 4$, then $J = 3$, for instance. Additionally, probabilistic step functions can assume many forms, each corresponding to the defined characteristics of polytomous IRT models: graded response, partial credit, or alternatives such as adjacent categories (see Muraki & Bock, 2003; Samejima, 1997). But the most common DSF uses a cumulative model.

The DSF framework addresses the amount of difference between the focal and reference groups at each step. This primary DSF feature is readily seen when the functions are plotted for visual inspection, as is displayed in Figure 11.1 for a four-response (hence, three-step-function) polytomous item. The plot has customary IRT scaling for the X and Y axes. Note the six lines, two for each step, and considering each step, one line each represents the function for the reference and focal groups. In this illustration, the lines are sufficiently close so that the inference may be drawn by the eye of no DSF at any of the steps. When a statistical test is needed, a delta statistic is useful to evaluate the null hypothesis of no DIF. However, appreciate, too, that the probability (Y axis) crosses between Steps 1 and 2, indicating that a mix of proficiency is observed in proficiency between these steps. Additional information about the step function is revealed by observing the close proximity of proficiency from Step 1 to Step 2 and the much further proximity (i.e., higher on the proficiency scale; X axis) from these steps to Step 3. This useful information is revealed in the DSF methodology. An approachable NCME (National Council on Measurement in Education) instructional module on DSF is available from Penfield and Gattamorta (2009).

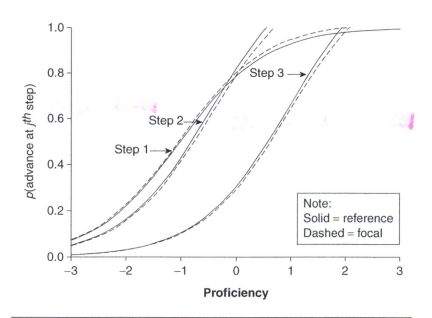

Figure 11.1   Illustrative Step Function in Polytomous Item DIF Analysis

Computer-Based Testing

Delivering a test on a computer screen is common in many small-scale circumstances and is used with limited success in some large-scale programs. Frequently, with computer-based testing, the on-screen test is identical or nearly identical to the paper-and-pencil version and often does not incorporate IRT scaling or other aspects of more complex computer applications such as computer-adaptive testing (CAT) or "tailored" testing (see discussion below). There are many design options for computer-based testing. The advantage of delivering a test on a computer screen, of course, is that scoring can be immediate and changes to the test itself can be efficiently made when developing alternative forms. A central concern with computer-based testing is the security of the testing environment when administration is remotely done.

Importantly, regardless of these advantages and disadvantages, there is a wide body of research on testing by computer, which suggests that the assessment is fundamentally changed by this delivery mechanism (see Mills, Portenza, Fremer, & Ward, 2002). Be advised that computer-based testing is fraught with psychometric challenges, and persons considering the use of computer-based testing should become familiar with current research so that they may be well informed before attempting to put this mode of administration into practice. A meta-analysis of some comparison literature is offered by Wang, Jiao, Young, Brooks, and Olson (2008).

Despite these concerns, DIF investigation for computer-based tests can proceed, and often with or without modification, by any of the described DIF methods. Zwick (2000) warns, too, that the mode itself may be a source of error in measurement. Thus, persons involved with computer-based testing may consider exploring differences between paper-and-pencil versus computer-based administration as the sorting variable for the focal and reference groups in a DIF analysis.

Computer-Adaptive Testing

CAT is a developing science and a growing practice in the current assessment scene. van der Linden and Glas (2000) describe CAT as follows:

> Instead of giving each examinee the same fixed tests, CAT item selection adapts to the ability level of individual examinees. After each response the examinee's ability estimate is updated and the subsequent item is selected to have optimal properties at the new estimate. (p. vii)

By this scheme, then, the number of items presented to an examinee is particular to that individual and depends on his or her responses to the previous set of items. Only when a consistent pattern of responses relative to the characteristics of the items is detected does the iterative routine halt. Imaginably, examinees respond with varying degrees of consistency, and hence, the number of items needed to reach a criterion for ability estimation also differs.

With sometimes more or fewer items, the worth of each item's contribution to the developed score is heightened when compared with tests in which all items are presented to every examinee. Because of this, examining for DIF may be more important in CAT than in nonadaptive tests, and any flawed item may be more consequential to the score (Zwick, 2000).

As can be readily imagined, exploring item function with DIF methods in CAT is extraordinarily difficult, fraught with both technical challenges and pitfalls in interpretation. Nonetheless, it is important for a number of reasons. First, of course, is to understand the DIF phenomenon itself. Also, DIF may appear more pronounced in CAT than in traditional paper-and-pencil presentations as only certain items are presented to the examinee. When item presentation is confounded with aberrant functioning due to nontest concerns, DIF may be difficult to accurately detect and interpret.

Translated Tests

The notion of using DIF to detect flaws in items translated from one language to another—or even across cultures—has been extant since early research on test item bias (Allalouf et al., 1999; Brislin, 1970; Hulin, Drasgow, & Komocar, 1982); however, it is infrequently used. Regardless, this use of DIF analysis can be effective and useful. Hambleton (1993) proffers an example in a Swedish-English translated test where the target item uses the English words "webbed feet" in describing the characteristic of some birds. The intent of the item is for the examinee to identify a suitable habitat for such birds. When translated into Swedish, however, the words become "swimming feet," which gives a direct and obvious clue to the correct response. Thus, the item is not equivalent to the two language groups, and the resultant cultural comparisons on the assessment cannot be reliably made.

It appears, too, that no single DIF detection strategy is more suited for use with translated test or when the intent is to make cross-cultural comparisons. The primary concern when the focus is cultural differences is whether the DIF method would be appropriate for the specific testing context and information sought.

Furthermore, as more tests are translated, with some new ones being developed with specification for multilanguage contexts, it is important to explore DIF. International organizations such as the International Test Commission even offer guidelines to assist persons in this specialized research (Hambleton, 1994). We encourage people to work with tests that may be used in cross-cultural contexts, and certainly tests that may be translated, to explore DIF by an appropriate strategy.

Additionally, when increasing attention on assessment of persons of varying ethnicities or cultural backgrounds, this application of DIF detection methodologies can also be usefully employed in test and item development (see Gierl, Rogers, & Klinger, 1999).

CHAPTER 12. FUTURE DIRECTIONS

As we noted in our introduction, the field of DIF research is fertile and growing. We see through these chapters that DIF investigation strategies and methods are evolving and new ones are being invented. Some procedures of special note are discussed in the previous chapter on specialized approaches to DIF. Looking ahead, we find that IRT-based DIF methods are evolving. This IRT perspective was foreshadowed by Thissen et al. (1993), who noted that modern DIF analyses can be viewed as a special case of multiple-group IRT, where groups are composed of the focal variables (e.g., gender, race/ethnicity).

Validity Argument

An additional new direction of DIF work is to investigate items as a prescriptive application of the validity argument. This approach is termed *item validation* (Kane, 2006; Lissitz & Samuelsen, 2007). This perspective of DIF work directly and assertively supports modern notions of validity as an evaluative argument, as put forth by American Educational Research Association et al. (1999) in *The Standards for Educational and Psychological Testing* and by important proponents like Messick (1988, 1989). Here, validity is firmly viewed as making supportable (and usually evidence based) statements about the meaningfulness, utility, and appropriateness of interpretations derived from test scores in a particular assessment situation. This explanation for validity is widely recognized among psychometricians and other professionals working in measurement but regretfully still remains largely unappreciated by many others who also work with tests, including some teachers, policymakers, and even nescient test developers.

The validity argument approach seems to be founded in the original validity work of Gulliksen (1950), who theorized test validity as a kind of agreement between the item and the test (measured as a biserial correlation), and is apparently consistent with notions for the role of items in tests put forth by Lord (1980), who stated that "the contribution of a single item depends in an intricate way on the choice of items included in the test" (p. 72).

Muthen (1988) calls this kind of investigation "micro-level test validity" and recommends that it be studied as a confirmatory factor issue, using structural equation modeling.

Osterlind (2006) with concurrence from others (see Haladyna, 1999) has drawn attention to the fact that test interpretation stems from item information; hence, validity evidence for a whole test presupposes appropriate and meaningful inferences derived from items. From this, it can be seen that when establishing a validity argument for DIF, examining data from examinee responses alone is inadequate. Additional sources, such as expert content examination by appropriate specialists and a careful link for an item to a content specification, should be included.

Null Hypothesis Testing

Closely related to the validity argument in DIF and, as noted earlier, one perspective on DIF that is gaining attention is that of null hypothesis testing for aberrant item identification. This approach fits neatly with evolving conceptions of validity as test score interpretation. Paul Holland and his colleagues at the Educational Testing Service (Dorans & Holland, 1993; Holland & Wainer, 1993) developed this evaluative argument. Using the M-H method, DIF is assessed using the standard null hypothesis testing approach, with the null hypothesis representing the absence of DIF in the studied test item. That is to say, in this framework the null hypothesis suggests that an item's characteristic of "difficulty" is independent of group membership (i.e., the reference or focal group) at a given score level. Conversely, the alternative hypothesis is that there is, indeed, a more uniform (or homogeneous) conditional dependence between the items' characteristics and group membership, suggesting the presence of DIF in the studied item(s).

A number of researchers (see Cohen, Kane, & Crooks, 1998; Tryon, 2001) have repeatedly pointed to the uses and misuses of null hypothesis testing in educational and psychological research, and their admonitions are beginning to take hold in studies of DIF (Casabianca, 2008; Wells et al., 2008). More recently, DIF researchers are employing tests for equivalence by using two one-sided tests approach, as outlined by Markus (2001), Tryon (2001), and Wellek (2002). Generally, this approach modifies the traditional null hypothesis framework to include two sets of alternative values that conjointly define "difference" and one set of interval values to define "equivalence," thus using two one-sided tests.

Statistical Modeling (HLM and Other)

Increasingly in educational and psychological research, statistical modeling is employed to evaluate a phenomenon. This viewpoint is extending to DIF analyses as well. We have already seen this position earlier in IRT-based approaches, with their focus on the latency of the variable. For statistical modeling with DIF, the consideration of group differences in performance is extended to regard a particular set of items as a random sample from a broader category of test stimuli. When doing so, logistic mixed models are employed such that uniform DIF is modeled to treat item effects and their interaction as random, rather than the usual perspective of them being fixed. In parallel fashion, groups' effects can be also modeled as random. When doing so, the groups are treated as randomly selected from a population consisting of a larger number of groups.

Such modeling approaches to DIF exploration give occasion to study possible explanations and even determine causes. The possible explanations are added as covariates to the model. Thus, the DIF is conditioned on group variables or item characteristics. It is useful to note that by this arrangement of conditioning effects, the explanations need not be complete or perfect; regardless, some useful (and often very meaningful) information is still obtained.

In the IRT approaches to this modeling, the ogive of the ICC (function) varies over groups, and both the location (i.e., difficulty) and the slope (i.e., discrimination) parameters display the model. This conception fits well with IRT models, which are generally thought of as logistic mixed models (see Adams, Wilson, & Wu, 1997; Bock & Aitkin, 1981).

Van den Noortgate and de Boeck (2005) demonstrate the random approach to be viable in several practical testing contexts, citing three advantages: (1) logistic models are both flexible in accommodating many circumstances as well as readily understood by knowledgeable practitioners; (2) they are statistically more economical since only parameter means and variances are estimated, instead of all individual effects separately; and (3) hypothesized causes and further explanations can be accommodated as covariates, even providing for their incompleteness and imperfections.

Applications of hierarchical linear modeling (HLM) to DIF statistical modeling are relatively new to DIF investigation but show great promise for meaningful analyses. In HLM, the aberrant item function phenomenon is modeled as a two-level formation of response to an item. Ability is modeled as a random effect, rather than used to calibrate item parameters as is done in IRT. Stochastic parts of HLM (e.g., random coefficients) are considered part of normal measurement error and are deemphasized when employing HLM in DIF work. This approach is young but growing with recent attention on HLM approaches in many contexts. Kamata (2001) is notably doing exploratory research in this area.

Equivalence Testing

In a recent article by Wells et al. (2008), the equivalence testing approach was employed to detect DIF using IRT-based methods based on Lord's chi-square. Using relatively large sample sizes, they demonstrated the utility of equivalence testing in a DIF framework and found the approach to be relatively robust to changes in test length. In an extension of this work, Casabianca (2008) developed an approach she coined as "equivalent item functioning" (EIF), using the two one-sided tests method (Tryon, 2001; Wellek, 2002).

Using simulated data from a one-parameter (Rasch) model, Casabianca (2008) varied sample sizes and DIF levels to examine the robustness of the EIF method for the M-H estimators. She concluded that this novel EIF approach, though somewhat stringent, is viable for DIF detection and offers an advantage to traditional DIF methods because it provides information about whether a test item performs equivalently across subgroups of examinees.

DFIT and CDIF Testing

In another novel direction, the DFIT methodology developed by Raju (1988) and his colleagues offers another powerful and flexible approach to assessing DIF. The DFIT method, for example, can be used for assessing DIF in both dichotomous and polytomous test items, and it has been used to assess both unidimensional and multidimensional tests. DFIT statistics are derived from IRT parameter estimates and, consequently, require relatively large sample sizes for parameter estimation. In addition to providing the standard estimates of DIF at the item level, this approach also provides estimates of both compensatory (CDIF) and noncompensatory DIF (NCDIF). Perhaps more usefully, the DFIT approach offers the advantage of assessing DTF as well.

The idea of compensatory DIF, as represented by the CDIF index, has the advantage of allowing researchers to study the overall effect of removing particular test items on the estimation of DTF, the differential functioning of the test as a whole. Thus, within this framework, test developers and psychometric specialists may be able to develop tests with the least amount of differential impact at the test score level.

Raju et al. (1995) initially devised significance tests for DFIT based on the χ^2 statistic. The central idea was to develop statistical tests for identifying CDIF, and ultimately DTF. These χ^2 tests have, over time, been refined and a relatively novel item parameter replication method has been proposed recently (Oshima, Raju, & Nanda, 2006). Perhaps more important for researchers is the fact that these new innovations have been implemented in the current version of the DFIT software programs (see Raju et al., 2005). For more details on the technical underpinnings of DFIT, the reader is referred to Oshima et al. (2006).

As can be seen, these methods point to ever more DIF-related work, both in applied settings and in the development of new methods.

CONCLUSION

We can see that the entire concept of investigating differences in performance between groups has undergone enormous changes over the past decades. The idea of DIF is conceived more broadly than before, including notions about fairness, bias, adverse impact, and more that are now integral to the topic. The procedures used to investigate the phenomenon of systematic group differences have evolved, with new ones invented and inadequate ones discarded. Working from a practical perspective, we describe and explain a number of common and important statistical approaches for detecting DIF. Our goal throughout was to update and highlight the important changes that have taken place in this area of applied statistics over the past quarter-century, since the earlier edition, *Test Item Bias*, was published in 1983. This topic is vast, and from our broader, more modern statistical vantage point, our aim has been to present current thinking and research, although we offer a little of the history, too, as this is useful in gaining complete understanding of the topic. In this brief monograph, we make no attempt to be comprehensive, nor do we suggest that what we write is definitive. To that end, we offer numerous citations to current and important works by many others. As can be seen from our reference list, exploration in the field of DIF in mental measures benefits from attention by many researchers. Collectively, they continue to add new and useful knowledge and ever-better techniques to DIF investigation, and their work will advance the field. We hope that this monograph provides useful information to researchers, scholars, students, test developers, and others as they explore the important field of DIF in modern measurement.

REFERENCES

Ackerman, T. (1992). A didactic explanation of item bias, item impact, and item validity from a multidimensional perspective. *Journal of Educational Measurement, 29,* 674–691.

Adams, R. J., Wilson, M., & Wu, M. (1997). Multilevel item response models: An approach to error in variables regression. *Journal of Educational and Behavioral Statistics, 22*(1), 47–76.

Allalouf, A., Hambleton, R. K., & Sireci, S. G. (1999). Identifying the causes of DIF in translated verbal items. *Journal of Educational Measurement, 36*(3), 185–198.

American Educational Research Association, American Psychological Association, & National Council on Measurement in Education. (1999). *Standards for educational and psychological testing.* Washington, DC: American Educational Research Association.

Angoff, W. H. (1993). Perspective on differential item functioning methodology. In P. W. Holland & W. Wainer (Eds.), *Differential item functioning* (pp. 3–24). Baltimore: Johns Hopkins University Press.

Baker, F. B. (2001). *The basics of item response theory.* Retrieved May 5, 2009, from http://echo.edres.org:8080/irt/baker/

Berk, R. A. (Ed.). (1982). *Handbook of methods for detecting item bias.* Baltimore: Johns Hopkins University Press.

Birnbaum, A. (1958). *On the estimation of mental abilities* (Series Report No 115. Project 7755-23). Randolf Air Force Base, TX: USAF School of Aviation Medicine.

Birnbaum, A. (1968). *Some latent trait models and their use in inferring an examinee's ability.* In F. M. Lord & M. R. Novick (Eds.), *Statistical theories of mental test scores* (pp. 395–479). Reading, MA: Addison-Wesley.

Bock, R. D., & Aitkin, M. (1981). Marginal maximum likelihood estimation of item parameters: Application of an EM algorithm. *Psychometrika, 46,* 443–445.

Bolt, D. M. (2002). A Monte Carlo comparison of parametric and nonparametric polytomous DIF detection methods. *Applied Measurement in Education, 15,* 113–141.

Bolt, D. M. (2005). Limited and full-information IRT estimation. In A. Maydeu-Olivares & J. McArdie (Eds.), *Contemporary psychometrics* (pp. 27–71). Hillsdale, NJ: Lawrence Erlbaum.

Brislin, R. W. (1970). Back-translation for cross-cultural research. *Journal of Cross-Cultural Psychology, 1,* 185–216.

Camilli, G. (2006). Test fairness. In R. L. Brennan (Ed.), *Educational measurement* (4th ed., pp. 220–256). Westport, CT: American Council on Education.

Camilli, G., & Shepard, L. (1994). *Methods for identifying biased test items.* Thousand Oaks, CA: Sage.

Casabianca, J. M. (2008). *Equivalence testing for differential item function detection.* Unpublished draft of master of arts thesis, Fordham University, New York.

Clauser, B. E., & Mazor, K. M. (1998). Using statistical procedures to identify differential item functioning test items. *Educational Measurement: Issues and Practice, 17,* 31–44.

Cleary, T. A. (1968). Test bias: Prediction of grades of Negro and White students in integrated colleges. *Journal of Educational Measurement, 5,* 115–124.

Clifford, H. W. (1982). Simpson's Paradox in real life. *The American Statistician, 36,* 46–48.

Cohen, A. S., Kane, M. T., & Crooks, T. J. (1998). A generalized examinee-centered method for setting standards on achievement tests. *Applied Psychological Measurement, 12,* 343–366.

Cole, N., & Moss, P. (1989). Bias in test use. In R. L. Linn (Ed.), *Educational measurement* (3rd ed.). New York: American Council on Education/Macmillan.

Cole, N. S. (1993). History and development of DIF. In P. W. Holland & H. Wainer (Eds.), *Differential item functioning* (p. 25). Hillsdale, NJ: Lawrence Erlbaum.

Dodeen, H., & Johanson, G. A. (2003). An analysis of sex-related differential item functioning in attitude assessment. *Assessment and Evaluation in Higher Education, 28,* 129–134.

Dorans, N. J., & Holland, P. W. (1993). DIF detection and description. In P. W. Holland & H. Wainer (Eds.), *Differential item functioning* (pp. 35–66). Hillsdale, NJ: Lawrence Erlbaum.

Dorans, N. J., & Kulick, E. (1983). *Assessing unexpected differential item performance of female candidates on SAT and TSWE forms administered in December 1977: An application of the standardization approach* (Research Report No. 83–9). Princeton, NJ: Educational Testing Service.

Dorans, N. J., & Kulick, E. (1986). Demonstrating the utility of the standardization approach to assessing unexpected differential item performance on the SAT. *Journal of Educational Measurement, 23,* 355–368.

Drasgow, F. (1987). Study of the measurement bias of two standardized psychological tests. *Journal of Applied Psychology, 72,* 19–29.

du Toit, M. (Ed.). (2003). *IRT from SSI: BILOG-MG, MULTILOG, PARSCALE, TESTFACT.* Lincolnwood, IL: Scientific Software International. Retrieved May 5, 2009, from www.ssicentral.com

Embretson, S. E., & Reise, S. P. (2000). *Item response theory for psychologists.* Mahwah, NJ: Lawrence Erlbaum.

Fildago, A. M., Ferreres, D., & Muniz, J. (2005). Liberal and conservative differential item functioning detection using Mantel-Haenszel and SIBTEST: Implications for Type I and Type II error rates. *Journal of Experimental Education, 73,* 23–39.

Finch, H. (2005). The MIMIC model as a method for detecting DIF: Comparison with Mantel-Haenszel, SIBTEST, and the IRT likelihood ratio. *Applied Psychological Measurement, 29,* 278–295.

Flowers, C. P., Oshima, T. C., & Raju, N. S. (1999). A description and demonstration of the polytomous-DFIT framework. *Applied Psychological Measurement, 23*(4), 309–326.

French, A. W., & Miller, T. R. (1996). Logistic regression and its use in detecting differential item functioning in polytomous items. *Journal of Educational Measurement, 33,* 315–332.

Gelin, M. N., Carelton, B. C., Smith, A. A., & Zumbo, B. D. (2004). The dimensionality and gender differential item functioning of the mini asthma quality of life questionnaire (MINIAQLQ). *Social Indicators Research, 68,* 91–105.

Gierl, M., Gotzmann, A., & Boughton, K. A. (2004). Performance of SIBTEST when the percentage of DIF items is large. *Applied Measurement in Education, 17*(3), 241–264.

Gierl, M. J., Rogers, W. T., & Klinger, D. (1999). *Using statistical and judgmental reviews to identify and interpret translation DIF.* Paper presented at the National Council on Measurement in Education, New Orleans, LA.

Gulliksen, H. (1950). *Theory of mental tests.* New York: Wiley.

Guttman, L. (1950). The basis for scalogram analysis. In S. A. Stouffer et al. (Eds.), *Measurement and prediction: The American soldier* (Vol. IV). New York. Wiley.

78

Haladyna, T. M. (1999). *Developing and validating multiple-choice test items* (2nd ed.). Mahwah, NJ: Lawrence Erlbaum.

Hambleton, R. K. (1993). Translating achievement tests for use in cross-cultural studies. *Journal of Psychological Assessment, 9,* 57–68.

Hambleton, R. K. (1994). Guidelines for adapting educational and psychological tests: A progress report. *European Journal of Psychological Assessment, 10,* 229–244.

Hambleton, R. K., & Bollward, J. (1990). *Factors affecting the stability of Mantel-Haenszel item bias statistics.* Amherst: University of Massachusetts.

Hambleton, R. K., & Swaminathan, H. (1985). *Item response theory: Principles and applications.* Boston: Kluwer-Nijoff.

Hambleton, R. K., Swaminathan H., & Rogers, J. H. (1991). *Fundamentals of item response theory.* Newbury Park, CA: Sage.

Holland, P. W. (1985). *On the study of differential item performance without IRT.* Paper presented at the Proceedings of the Military Testing Association.

Holland, P. W., & Thayer, D. T. (1988). Differential item functioning and the Mantel-Haenszel procedure. In H. Wainer & H. I. Braun (Eds.), *Test validity* (pp. 129–145). Hillsdale, NJ: Lawrence Erlbaum.

Holland, P. W., & Wainer, H. (1993). *Differential item functioning.* Hillsdale, NJ: Lawrence Erlbaum.

Hosmer, D. W., & Lemeshow, S. (1989). *Applied logistic regression.* New York: Wiley.

Hulin, C. L., Drasgow, F., & Komocar, J. (1982). Applications of item response theory to analysis of attitude scale translations. *Journal of Applied Psychology, 67,* 818–825.

Jensen, A. R. (1980). *Bias in mental testing.* New York: Free Press.

Kamata, A. (2001). Item analysis by the hierarchical generalized linear model. *Journal of Educational Measurement, 38*(1), 79–93.

Kane, M. T. (2006). Validation. In R. L. Brennan (Ed.), *Educational measurement* (4th ed., pp. 17–64). Westport, CT: Praeger.

Klockars, A. J., & Lee, Y. (2008). Simulated tests of differential item functioning using SIBTEST with and without impact. *Journal of Educational Measurement, 45*(3), 271–285.

Koretz, D., & Hamilton, L. S. (2006). Testing for accountability in K-12. In R. L. Brennan (Ed.), *Educational measurement* (4th ed., pp. 531–578). Westport, CT: American Council on Education/Praeger.

Kwak, N., Davenport, E. D., & Davison, M. L. (1998, April). *A comparative study of observed score approaches and purification procedures for detecting differential item functioning.* Paper presented at the National Council on Measurement in Education, Denver, CO.

Lane, S., & Stone, C. A. (2006). Performance assessments. In R. L. Brennan (Ed.), *Educational measurement* (4th ed., pp. 422–468). Westport, CT: American Council on Education/ Praeger.

Lange, R., Thalbourne, M. A., Houran, J., & Lester, D. (2002). Depressive response sets due to gender and culture-based differential item functioning. *Personality and Individual Differences, 33,* 937–954.

Lissitz, R. W., & Samuelsen, K. (2007). A suggested change in terminology and emphasis regarding validity and education. *Educational Researcher, 36,* 437–448.

Lord, F. M. (1980). *Applications of item response theory to practical testing problems.* Hillsdale, NJ: Lawrence Erlbaum.

Lord, F. M., & Novick, M. R. (1968). *Statistical theories of mental test scores.* Reading, MA: Addison-Wesley.

Mantel, N., & Haenszel, W. (1959). Statistical aspects of the analysis of data from retrospective studies of disease. *Journal of the National Cancer Institute, 22,* 719–748.

Markus, K. A. (2001). The converse of inequality argument against tests of statistical significance. *Psychological Methods, 6,* 147–160.

Mellenbergh, G. J. (1982). Contingency table models for assessing item bias. *Journal of Educational Statistics, 7,* 105–118.

Messick, S. (1988). The once and future issues of validity: Assessing the meaning and consequences of measurement. In H. Wainer & H. I. Braun (Eds.), *Test validity* (pp. 33–46). Hillsdale, NJ: Lawrence Erlbaum.

Messick, S. (1989). Validity. In R. L. Linn (Ed.), *Educational measurement* (3rd ed., pp. 13–105). New York: American Council on Education/Macmillan.

Mills, C. N., Portenza, M. T., Fremer, J. J., & Ward, W. C. (2002). *Computer-based testing.* Mahwah, NJ: Lawrence Erlbaum.

Millsap, R. E., & Everson, H. T. (1993). Methodological review: Statistical approaches for assessing measurement bias. *Applied Psychological Measurement, 17*(4), 297–334.

Muraki, E. (1992). *RESGEN* (No. RR-92–7). Princeton, NJ: Educational Testing Service.

Muraki, E., & Bock, D. (2003). *PARSCALE: IRT based test scoring and item analysis for graded response items and rating scales* (Version 4.1). Lincolnwood, IL: Scientific Software International.

Muthen, B. O. (1988). Some uses of structural equation modeling in validity studies: Extending IRT to external variables. In H. Wainer & H. I. Braun (Eds.), *Test validity.* Mahwah, NJ: Lawrence Erlbaum.

Oshima, T. C., Raju, N. S., & Nanda, A. O. (2006). A new method for assessing the statistical significance in the differential functioning of items and tests (DFIT) framework. *Journal of Educational Measurement, 43,* 1–17.

Osterlind, S. J. (1983). *Test item bias* (Vol. 30). Beverly Hills, CA: Sage.

Osterlind, S. J. (2006). *Modern measurement: Theory, principles, and applications of mental appraisal.* Upper Saddle River, NJ: Prentice Hall.

Osterlind, S. J., Sheng, Y., Wang, Z., Beaujean, A. A., & Nagel, T. (2008). *Technical manual: College Basic Subjects Examination.* Columbia: University of Missouri-Columbia.

Penfield, R. D., & Camilli, G. (2007). Differential item functioning and item bias. In C. R. Rao & S. Sinharay (Eds.), *Handbook of statistics* (Vol. 26, pp. 125–167). New York: Elsevier.

Penfield, R. D., & Gattamorta, K. (2009). An NCME instructional module using differential step functioning to refine the analyis of DIF in polytomous items. *Educational Measurement: Issues and Practice, 28*(1), 38–49.

Penfield, R. D., & Lam, T. C. M. (2000). Assessing differential item functioning in performance assessment: Review and recommendations. *Educational Measurement Issues and Practice, 19*(3), 5–15.

Potenza, M. T., & Dorans, N. J. (1995). DIF assessment for polytomously scored items: A framework for classification and evaluation. *Applied Psychological Measurement, 19,* 23–37.

Raju, N. S. (1988). The area between two item characteristic curves. *Psychometrika, 53,* 495–502.

Raju, N. S., Oshima, T. C., & Wolach, A. (2005). Differential functioning of items and tests (DFIT): Dichotomous and polytomous [Computer program]. Chicago: Illinois Institute of Technology.

Raju, N. S., van der Linden, W. J., & Fleer, P. F. (1995). IRT-based internal measures of differential functioning of items and tests. *Applied Psychological Measurement, 19*(4), 153–168.

Rasch, G. (1960). *Probabilistic models for some intelligence and attainment tests.* Copenhagen, Denmark: Denmark Pedagogiske Institute. (Reprinted in 1980, Chicago: University of Chicago Press)

Roussos, L. A., & Stout, W. F. (1996). A multidimensionality-based DIF analysis paradigm. *Applied Psychological Measurement, 20,* 355–371.

Rudner, L., & Gagne, P. (2001). An overview of three approaches to scoring written essays by computer. *Practical Assessment, Research & Evaluation, 7*(26). Retrieved May 5, 2009, from http://ericae.net/pare/getvn.asp?v=7&n=26

Samejima, F. (1997). Graded response model. In W. J. van der Linden & R. K. Hambleton (Eds.), *Handbook of modern item response theory* (pp. 67–84). New York: Springer.

Shealy, R., & Stout, W. (1993). A model-based standardization approach that separates true bias/DIF from group ability differences and detects test bias/DIF as well as item bias/DIF. *Psychometrika, 58,* 159–194.

Shepard, L., Camilli, G., & Averil, M. (1981). Comparison of procedures for detecting test-item bias with both internal and external ability criteria. *Journal of Educational Statistics, 6,* 317–375.

Simpson, E. H. (1951). The interpretation of interaction in contingency tables. *Journal of the Royal Statistical Society B, 13,* 238–241.

SPSS. (2008). SPSS 16.0 for Windows (Version 16.0). Chicago: Author.

Stout, W. (1995). SIBTEST: Differential items/bundle functioning. St. Paul, MN: Assessment Systems Corporation.

Thissen, D., Chen, W., & Bock, D. (2003). MULTILOG: multiple category item analysis and test scoring using item response theory (Version 7) . Lincolnwood, IL: Scientific Software International.

Thissen, D., Steinberg, L., & Wainer, H. (1988). Use of item response theory in the study of group differences in trace lines. In H. Wainer & H. I. Braun (Eds.), *Test validity* (pp. 147–170). Hillsdale, NJ: Lawrence Erlbaum.

Thissen, D., Steinberg, L., & Wainer, H. (1993). Detection of differential item functioning using the parameters of item response models. In P. W. Holland & H. Wainer (Eds.), *Differential item functioning* (pp. 67–113). Hillsdale, NJ: Lawrence Erlbaum.

Tryon, W. W. (2001). Evaluating statistical difference, equivalence, and indeterminancy using inferential confidence intervals: An integrated alternative method of conducing null hypothesis statistical tests. *Psychological Methods, 6*(4), 371–386.

van den Noortgate, W., & De Boeck, P. (2005). Assessing and explaining differential item functioning using logistic models. *Journal of Educational and Behavioral Statistics, 30*(4), 443–464.

van der Linden, W. J., & Glas, C. A. W. (Eds.). (2000). *Computerized adaptive testing: Theory and practice.* Boston: Kluwer.

Wang, S., Jiao, H., Young, M., Brooks, T., & Olson, J. (2008). Comparability of computer-based and paper-and-pencil testing in K–12 reading assessments. *Educational and Psychological Measurement, 68*(1), 5–24.

Wellek, S. (2002). *Testing statistical hypotheses of equivalence.* Boca Raton, FL: Chapman & Hall.

Wells, C. S., Wollack, J. A., & Serlin, R. C. (2008, April). *An equivalency test for model DIF.* Paper presented at the annual meeting of the National Council on Measurement in Education, New York.

Whitmore, M. L., & Schumacker, R. E. (1999). A comparison of logistic regression and analysis of variance differential item functioning detection methods. *Educational and Psychological Measurement, 59*(4), 910–927.

Wilder, G., & Powell, K. (1989). Sex differences in test performance: A survey of the literature (Report No. RR 89-4). Princeton, NJ: Educational Testing Service.

Williams, B. (1978). *A sampler on sampling.* New York: Wiley.

Wood, R., Wilson, D., Gibbons, R., Schilling, S., Muraki, E., & Bock, D. (2003). TESTFACT: Test scoring, item statistics, and item factor analysis (Version 4.0). Lincolnwood, IL: Scientific Software International.

Zieky, M. (2006). Fairness reviews in assessment. In S. M. Downing & T. M. Haladyna (Eds.), *Handbook of test development* (pp. 359–376). Mahwah, NJ: Lawrence Erlbaum.

Zumbo, B. (1999). *A handbook on the theory and methods of differential item functioning: Logistic regression modeling as a unitary framework for binary and Likert-type item scores.* Ottawa, Ontario, Canada: Directorate of Human Resources Research and Evaluation, National Defense Headquarters.

Zwick, R. (2000). The assessment of differential item functioning in computer adaptive tests. In W. J. van der Linden & C. A. W. Glas (Eds.), *Computerized adaptive testing: Theory and practice* (pp. 275–321). Boston: Kluwer.

Zwick, R., Donoghue, J. R., & Grima, A. (1993). Assessment of differential items functioning for performance tasks. *Journal of Educational Measurement, 30,* 233–251.

AUTHOR INDEX

SUBJECT INDEX

Made in the USA
Monee, IL
08 October 2021